THE LAUREL POETRY SERIES *is unique in the growing range of fine, inexpensive paperbound books. Each volume contains, along with an original introduction, biographical notes, a bibliography, and notes on the poetry.*

ANNE FERRY *received her Bachelor's and Master's degrees from Vassar College and her Ph.D. from Columbia University. Winner of a Fulbright scholarship to Girton College, Cambridge, she has taught at Hunter and Wellesley Colleges and is now lecturer in English at Harvard University. Mrs. Ferry is the author of "Milton's Epic Voice," a critical study, and is at present engaged in an anthology of 17th century religious literature and a book on later 17th century poetry.*

RICHARD WILBUR, *the General Editor, has won the Pulitzer Prize, the National Book Award, and the Millay Prize, all three in 1957 for his book of poems, "Things of This World." His most recent volume of poetry is "Advice to a Prophet." He has held a Guggenheim and a Prix de Rome Fellowship, and is a member of the National Institute of Arts and Letters. He is now Professor of English at Wesleyan University.*

The Laurel Poetry Series

General Editor, Richard Wilbur

17th Century English Minor Poets

Selected, with an introduction
and notes, by Anne D. Ferry

Published by
DELL PUBLISHING CO., INC.
750 Third Avenue
New York 17, New York

© *Copyright, 1964, by Richard Wilbur*

Laurel ® *TM 674623, Dell Publishing Co., Inc.*

Cover drawing by Richard Powers

First printing: November, 1964

Printed in U.S.A.

Contents

Introduction

When we read the seventeenth-century poetry included in this anthology, our attention is first caught by the remarkable number of particular poems that we feel to be among the finest lyrics in English literature—such poems as King's "The Exequy," Carew's "Ingrateful Beauty Threatened," Vaughan's "Peace," Cowley's "The Spring," James Shirley's "The glories of our blood and state," to name only a few. The large number of such poems of unmistakable excellence makes us wonder what it was in the nature of the period (Alfred North Whitehead called it the "century of genius") that inspired such lyric masterpieces. No other time in English history provided so many poets who could contribute single poems to distinguish a miscellany. We are almost seduced into accepting literally their metaphor of a presiding spirit, a muse, an Idea, mysteriously inspiring men of lesser gifts with miraculous moments of genius.

This sense of the seventeenth century as a remarkably fruitful period for poetry is also encouraged when we study not only individual lyrics but larger groups of poems by each of the ten poets emphasized in this anthology: Henry King, Thomas Carew, Sir John Suckling, Richard Lovelace, Abraham Cowley, Richard Crashaw, Henry Vaughan, Thomas Traherne, Edmund Waller, John Wilmot, Earl of Rochester. These writers—whose lives spanned the century—produced not only individual poems of the very highest order, but a large body of lyric verse of distinction and variety. Particularly Thomas Carew and Henry Vaughan had gifts that, in another age, might have earned them a more gratifying epithet than "minor."

It is, in fact, chiefly when we measure them against their contemporaries that we see their stature overshadowed by giants. We measure them by comparison to the two great innovators in lyric poetry at the beginning of the century —John Donne and Ben Jonson (the acknowledged masters of virtually all ten poets emphasized here); we compare them to the finest disciples of Donne and Jonson— George Herbert and Andrew Marvell (and, in some views, Robert Herrick); to their successor and critic—John Dryden; and finally to John Milton, the greatest poet of the century and virtually the only one who apparently owed nothing to the inventiveness of Jonson or Donne. In this context we see that Carew and Vaughan and the other poets selected here for emphasis were assuredly not among the first poets of their age (although many seventeenth-century readers, including Dryden and Rochester, might have ranked Cowley among the first), but we also recognize more sharply that the seventeenth century was a remarkable period in English literature, producing not only many individual lyrics of the highest order, but also an unusually large number of poets whose work as a whole demonstrates impressive fullness and power.

Various explanations have been offered for the literary plenitude of the seventeenth century: the unity of pre-scientific sensibility and language; the richness of the sacramental tradition as a source for metaphor; the enthusiasm for rediscovered ancient literary models; the fruitful influence of Jonson and Donne; the existence of a fit audience for poetry, with the leisure, training, and taste to enjoy it. Such explanations have taught us a great deal about seventeenth-century poetry—its characteristic excellences and limitations, its interconnections and its development. But like so many historical theories of literature, they describe the characteristic qualities of this poetry at least as much as they account for its historical origins. A theory about the historical causes of seventeenth-century poetry and of its development is a kind of description of *what it is;* a description of *what it is* can suggest what forces contributed to make it so.

To describe the characteristic qualities of seventeenth-century poetry is almost as difficult as to explain the historical forces that shaped it: as the poems collected in this anthology illustrate, a rich variety was characteristic of the period. We find love poetry and religious poetry, political verse, poems about other poems and about the nature of poetry. There are verses written upon public occasions—elegies on the death of Dr. Donne of St. Paul's by King and Carew, for example; and other poems upon intimate autobiographical matters, such as King's lines to his sister, Anne. There are love sonnets and songs imitating Italian and French forms of the sixteenth century. There are imitations of classical genres—epigram, epitaph, elegy, ode, epistle, epithalamium, and translations or adaptations of particular ancient poems, such as Rochester's "Upon Drinking in a Bowl" from Anacreon. There are poems written to be sung—in plays like Shirley's or as madrigals like Drummond's—and others written as if they were to be spoken by more than one voice, such as Crashaw's Nativity hymn, or the dialogues of Suckling, Townshend, and Davenant. We find poems of varying lengths, some in intricate stanza forms, others in couplets. Many poems allude to classical writings or medieval chivalric literature or Scripture or to all three. Often we find imagery drawn from nature (directly or through literary tradition)—from natural objects, like Lovelace's grasshopper and snail and Vaughan's waterfall, or from principles of nature such as growth, decline, regeneration. At other times the poets rely for their imagery upon music, geometry, astronomy, philosophy, theology, or magic. They demonstrate the influence of a variety of intellectual traditions—Crashaw of continental counter-Reformation movements, Vaughan of Hermetic interests which he shared with his brother Thomas, Traherne of science and the Neoplatonic strain in Christian thought, Cowley of Hobbesian rationalism, Rochester of scepticism and materialism, both ancient and modern. And especially we hear in this collection of poems almost every conceivable tone of voice—for example, Traherne's rapturous, Rochester's cynical, Crashaw's awed, Carew's intelligently urbane, Suckling's playful.

Any description of seventeenth-century poetry must acknowledge its rich variety. Yet it is possible to make some generalizations about the lyric in that period (granting, of course, that all such generalizations immediately suggest exceptions). It is possible to explain our sense that the hundred years represented in this volume are not marked off entirely arbitrarily, that these poets are related, despite their differences, by significant similarities. It is possible to recognize these poems as shaped by imaginations peculiar to one period of English literature —to distinguish them, for instance, from typical Elizabethan or Augustan or Romantic poetry. We can define the qualities that "The Exequy," "Ingrateful Beauty Threatened," "Peace," "The Spring," "The glories of our blood and state," and many other poems in this anthology share with still more famous lyrics of the seventeenth century—for example, with Donne's "The Sunrising" and Jonson's "This morning, timely rapt with holy fire," with Herbert's "Love," Marvell's "To His Coy Mistress," and Milton's sonnet upon his "late espoused saint."

These poems, different as they are, have in common an effect that identifies them as lyrics of the seventeenth rather than another century. It is an effect that is especially difficult to define, however, because these poems evoke in us simultaneously responses that other literature has taught us to think of as mutually exclusive or in some sense incompatible, contradictory. For the lyrics of this period dramatize particular events immediately happening to individual human beings, and yet dramatize them as they are included in and transformed by a world of timeless images or universal axioms, with the effect that what is personal, particular, individual, is seen at the same time—and with the same secure sense of reality —to be general and representative. It is a special fact about the seventeenth century that its poets could write of death or love or poetry with the immediately felt intensity that we associate with our individual experience (experience in time), and yet with the full authority, the secure generalizing power provided them by a world that was ideal, imagined, and therefore not limited by any particular time. We are made to respond to what is dramatized in such a poem—the parting of lovers, a seduction, someone meditating on death, a sinner's repentance —as if it were actually happening in time the way things happen in our own lives. Yet with no hesitation and with no loss of immediacy, we are made to respond to it as a timeless image or axiom that is true of all existence. Immediacy and universality do not demand different or contradictory responses from us nor do they diminish each other.

"A Contemplation Upon Flowers," usually attributed to Henry King, can illustrate this effect, which is quite different from the effect intended by a typical Elizabethan lyric on the same traditional theme, such as Thomas Nashe's "Litany in Time of Plague."

> Brave flowers, that I could gallant it like you
> And be as little vain;
> You come abroad, and make a harmless show,
> And to your beds of earth again;
> You are not proud, you know your birth
> For your embroidered garments are from earth.
>
> You do obey your months and times, but I
> Would have it ever spring;
> My fate would know no winter, never die
> Nor think of such a thing;
> Oh, that I could my bed of earth but view
> And smile, and look as cheerfully as you.
>
> Oh, teach me to see death and not to fear,
> But rather to take truce;
> How often have I seen you at a bier,
> And there look fresh and spruce;
> You fragrant flowers then teach me that my breath
> Like yours may sweeten, and perfume my death.

Unlike Nashe's "Litany," this is a dramatic poem, for it persuades us that something is happening, as we read it, to the particular person we hear speaking its lines; he seems to exist in time as we do. He is developing an argument or attitude leading to a conclusion, which therefore implies sequence and change that can occur only in time. He comes to this experience with knowledge of an existence extending beyond the limits of the poem, of a society that furnishes him metaphors for the flowers as young bloods, innocently foppish, "come abroad" to promenade in their "embroidered garments." His tone also contributes to the dramatic immediacy of the poem, because it conveys a sense of distinct personality. First we hear wistfulness and humility in his tribute to the flowers, curiously mixed with sophisticated awareness that their bravado is innocent because they lack his self-knowledge. His voice accumulates accents of self-mockery, fear, longing, a grim sense of incongruity (in "fresh and spruce"), and finally a quieter acceptance of the facts of dissolution and purification. This complexity of tone, and its accumulation of changes as we move toward the final lines, defines a distinct personality expressing his own recognition of death but—in the way of seventeenth-century lyrics—what we hear is at once the voice of a particular personality and the voice of *any* individual speaking for all men. The dramatic uses of structure, imagery, and tone create a speaker with the accents of a particular human being, but other uses of language endow him with the authority to represent and generalize for all men. Immediacy and universality are achieved at the same time, with no loss of authority or intensity.

The last two lines of the poem grow out of the imagery associated with the flowers. They refer to facts of the speaker's social experience—he has seen flowers at funerals and can expect them at his own. They complete his argument that the humility of the flowers in facing death is a lesson he must learn. They also express his deepening awareness that flowers can achieve humility at less cost, because, lacking individual identity, they escape individual mortality, and so will live on to sweeten his corpse. The final lines are therefore the climax of the poem's dramatic movement. Yet they have at the same time another effect, because they refer not only to the speaker's individual experience, but to the traditional doctrine of the odor of sanctity with which good deeds perfume the virtuous Christian's death. This reference completes a pattern of images in the poem that, without diminishing, transforms its dramatic effect because it redefines the speaker's world. If he sees the flowers as innocent fops, he also simultaneously sees them as Jesus in the Sermon on the Mount taught men to "Consider the lilies of the field;" and their cycle from birth to death in "beds of earth" reminds him that, like Adam, he was formed of dust to which he must return. This pattern of allusions, culminating in the final lines, transforms, without lessening, the dramatic effect of the poem, because we are made to see the speaker's world at the same time as a particular society and as a metaphor for any society, what Christian tradition calls "the World." The images of foppish elegance, implying the speaker's specific social experience in time, are seen also as metaphors for the vanity and pride of all men in all societies. The speaker himself, without losing his individuality, becomes representative of *any* individual; his final prayer is expressed in his own distinctive tone, and yet it is a prayer made for all men. It has authority as a generalization (comparable, for instance, to the closing couplet of Shirley's song in this anthology: "Only the actions of the just / Smell sweet, and blossom in their dust."). We acknowledge its general application without losing our sense of its personal force for the speaker who has discovered it. Because he dwells with secure knowledge in a particular social world and in an ideal, imagined world, he can use metaphors from either world to talk about the other. The effect is that he can generalize with the security we feel about individual knowledge, and yet in no way diminish the intensity of felt experience. We are therefore made to respond simultaneously to the immediacy of the speaker's acceptance of death and to its universality as a timeless axiom or image that is true for all human experience.

An analogy is provided by Waller's "Go, lovely rose" that can help to define the parallel effects created by otherwise dissimilar seventeenth-century lyrics. Like King, Waller chose a theme that had already attracted

Elizabethan poets, imitating Italian, French, and classical models. Yet "Go, lovely rose" creates an effect that parallels King's religious poem more closely than it resembles typical sixteenth-century persuasions to love, such as Christopher Marlowe's "Come live with me and be my love."

> Go, lovely rose!
> Tell her that wastes her time and me
> That now she knows,
> When I resemble her to thee,
> How sweet and fair she seems to be.
>
> Tell her that's young,
> And shuns to have her beauties spied,
> That hadst thou sprung
> In deserts where no men abide,
> Thou must have uncommended died.
>
> Small is the worth
> Of beauty from the light retired;
> Bid her come forth,
> Suffer herself to be desired,
> And not blush so to be admired.
>
> Then die! that she
> The common fate of all things rare
> May read in thee;
> How small a part of time they share,
> That are so wondrous sweet and fair!

Like "A Contemplation Upon Flowers," Waller's poem creates a dramatic effect, and by parallel means. We are persuaded that something is happening to the speaker; he seems to exist in time as we do ourselves. He has a past (implied by the occasion and his argument) and a future (which he hopes to enjoy with the lady). His language defines the particular society in which he lives, where beauties are "spied," where pretty young ladies are publicly "desired" and taught not to blush at such advances. His voice also indicates a distinct personality— for example, in the cynicism of "Small is the *worth*," the cruelty of "Then die!", the suave intelligence of the compliment. We never lose our sense of the speaker or his involvement in the immediate occasion, and yet, as in King's poem, the dramatic effect is finally transformed. The last stanza is the climax of the lover's argument and we hear in it his deepening accents of cruel passion and tenderness. But at the same time we also assent to the final lines as a truth about all mortal existence, a generalization that has universal application. They turn the particular occasion of the poem itself into an image, just as the speaker sees the particular rose and the individual girl as images of mortal beauty. The speaker's world is seen as a specific society but also as a metaphor for all civilized appreciation that would snatch youth, beauty, pleasure from the blankness of "deserts" and the indifference of time. Because for the speaker the social world and the world of timeless truth have equal reality, each can provide metaphors to talk about the other. The effect is significantly parallel to King's achievement because the speaker's generalizations about "all things rare," all mortal creatures that share "a part of time," are authoritative and moving. We feel them to be universally true, and not the less so because we are also aware of the immediate dramatic situation, even the irony of such large generalizations uttered to serve such private self-interest.

The effect that Waller's poem shares with "A Contemplation Upon Flowers" is the distinguishing mark of the seventeenth-century lyric. When, towards the end of the period, other qualities began to characterize poetry, what disappeared was not the capacity to relate individual human experiences to generalizations. Augustan poets could induce a general category from particular illustrations of it or interpret individual experiences as instances of general laws—habits of mind (displayed in some of the later poems in this anthology, especially by Traherne and Rochester) that were particularly suited to philosophical verse and to social satire. Romantic poets of the nineteenth and twentieth centuries, for whom the lyric again became the chief poetic expression, could explore in the truth of immediately felt experiences the possibility of finding universal truth or perhaps universal questions. What ceased to be true of lyric poetry by the end of the seventeenth century was the dramatic presentation of an event happening to an individual human being seen to live in time and in a society as we do, and yet seen to belong to a world that transforms the personal and individual into timeless images or axioms that have universal application. Peculiar to poets of this period was the sense that the particular social world and the ideal, imagined world have equal reality, that each can provide metaphors for the other without sacrifice of immediacy or authority. It was this fusion of dramatic particularity with secure generalizing power that stamped the finest achievements of minor seventeenth-century poets, and of their greater contemporaries, as creations of the "century of genius."

BIBLIOGRAPHY

WORKS:

The Poems of Bishop Henry King, ed. John Sparrow, London, 1925.

The Poems of Thomas Carew, ed. Rhodes Dunlap, Oxford, 1949.

The Works of Sir John Suckling, ed. A. H. Thompson, London, 1910.

The Poems of Richard Lovelace, ed. C. H. Wilkinson, Oxford, 1930.

The English Writings of Abraham Cowley, ed. A. R. Waller, Cambridge, 1905.

The Poems of Richard Crashaw, ed. L. C. Martin, Oxford, 1927.

The Works of Henry Vaughan, ed. L. C. Martin, Oxford, 1914.

Thomas Traherne's Centuries, Poems, and Thanksgivings, ed. H. M. Margoliouth, Oxford, 1958.

The Poems of Edmund Waller, ed. G. Thorn Drury, London, 1893.

Poems by John Wilmot, Earl of Rochester, ed. V. de Sola
Pinto, Cambridge, Mass., 1953.

CRITICISM:

Bennett, Joan. *Four Metaphysical Poets*, Cambridge,
1934.
Bush, Douglas. *English Literature of the Earlier Seven-
teenth Century*, Oxford, 1945.
Eliot, T. S. "The Metaphysical Poets," in *Selected Essays
1917–1932*, New York, 1960.
Grierson, H. J. C. *Metaphysical Lyrics and Poems of the
Seventeenth Century*, Oxford, 1921.
Johnson, Samuel. *The Lives of the English Poets*, ed. G.
B. Hill, Oxford, 1905.
Leavis, F. R. "The Line of Wit," in *Revaluation*, New
York, 1947.
Leishman, J. B. *The Metaphysical Poets*, Oxford, 1934.
Martz, L. I. *The Poetry of Meditation*, New Haven, 1954.
The Proper Wit of Poetry, Chicago, 1961.
Nicolson, Marjorie. *The Breaking of the Circle*, Evanston,
1950.
Sharp, R. L. *From Donne to Dryden*, Chapel Hill, 1940.
Tuve, Rosemond. *Elizabethan and Metaphysical Imagery*,
Chicago, 1947.
Walton, Geoffrey. *Metaphysical to Augustan*, London,
1955.
White, Helen. *The Metaphysical Poets*, New York, 1936.
Willey, Basil. *The Seventeenth Century Background*,
New York, 1950.
Williamson, George. *The Donne Tradition*, Cambridge,
Mass., 1930.

Biographical Notes

HENRY KING, born in 1592, was the son of the bishop who ordained John Donne. After his studies at Westminster and Christ Church, Oxford, he entered the church, became prebend of St. Paul's in 1616 and ultimately Bishop of Chichester in 1642. The next year he was ejected by the Puritans and not returned until the Restoration. He was executor of Donne's will and possibly the editor of the 1633 edition of Donne's poems. His own collected poems were published in 1657.

THOMAS CAREW was born in 1594/5, the son of a lawyer. After graduation from Merton College, Oxford, in 1611, he spent some time at the Middle Temple. He then acted as secretary to Sir Dudley Carleton on the continent, but was dismissed in 1616 for slandering his employer. In 1619 he travelled in the train of Edward Lord Herbert of Cherbury, ambassador to France, and in 1628 received an appointment at court, which he retained until his death (1639?). His masque, *Coelum Britannicum*, was presented and printed in 1634, his poems in 1640.

SIR JOHN SUCKLING was born of an old Norfolk family in 1609. He attended Trinity College, Cambridge and Gray's Inn, toured in Europe, and served under Gustavus Adolphus in 1631-32. He led a troop to Scotland in the first Bishop's War in 1639, and in 1641 took part in the plot to rescue Stafford from the Tower. Upon its discovery, he escaped to France, where he died (or possibly committed suicide) in 1642. His play, *Aglaura,* was produced in 1637/8; his poems, *Fragmenta Aurea,* were printed in 1646.

RICHARD LOVELACE, the son of a Kentish knight, was born in 1618. He was educated at Charterhouse (contemporary with Crashaw) and Oxford, then took up residence at court. He served in the Scottish expeditions of 1639 and 1640, and in 1642 presented to Parliament the Kentish petition in favor of episcopacy, for which he was imprisoned for seven weeks. He fought in England and under the French, in Holland, and in 1648 was again imprisoned for implication in royalist uprisings. He died in 1656 or 1657. *Lucasta* was published in 1649, *Lucasta: Posthume Poems* in 1660.

ABRAHAM COWLEY was born in London in 1618. He studied at Westminster and Trinity College, Cambridge, where he became a fellow in 1640. Before he could be forcibly ejected, he left in 1643 to join the court at Oxford. For ten years in France he was secretary to the queen and a royalist agent, but in 1654 he returned to England and the following year was imprisoned briefly. He began medical studies at Oxford, receiving his M. D. in 1657. After another sojourn in France, at the Restoration he was reinstated in his fellowship and presented by the queen with some land, to which he retired. He died in 1667. *Poetical Blossoms* was first published in 1633, *The Mistress* in 1647, *Poems* in 1656.

RICHARD CRASHAW was born in 1612/13, the son of William Crashaw, preacher at the Temple. He studied at the Charterhouse and Pembroke College, Cambridge, becoming a fellow of Peterhouse in 1635. He took part in the religious life of Little Gidding and was ordained by 1639, when he left Cambridge before being ejected by the Puritans. After some time on the continent, he was converted to Roman Catholicism, probably in 1645, and in 1647 he was in the service of Cardinal Pallotta, who appointed him to a post at the shrine of Loreto, where he died in 1649. His sacred epigrams were published in 1634, *Steps to the Temple* in 1646 (enlarged in 1648), and *Carmen Deo Nostro* in 1652.

HENRY VAUGHAN was born in Wales in 1621/22. With his twin brother, Thomas, he entered Jesus College, Oxford, in 1638, but after two years was sent to London to study law. After his service on the royalist side during the Civil War he turned to medical studies, and practised in Wales until his death in 1695. His first *Poems* were published in 1646, *Olor Iscanus* in 1651, *Silex Scintillans* in 1650 and 1655, *Thalia Rediviva* in 1678.

THOMAS TRAHERNE, born c. 1637, was the son of a Hereford shoemaker. He was educated at Brasenose College, Oxford, and received the living of Credenhill, Herefordshire, in 1657. After ten years spent there and at Oxford, he was made chaplain to Sir Orlando Bridgeman, Lord Keeper of the Seals, with whom he went into retirement at Teddington in 1672. He died there in 1674. Traherne's poems were unknown until published in 1903 by Bertram Dobell, who in 1908 printed the prose *Centuries of Meditations*.

EDMUND WALLER was born in 1606 of an ancient and wealthy family. He studied at Eton and King's College, Cambridge, and entered Parliament at sixteen. In 1631 he married an heiress, who died within three years, after which he paid court in verse to Lady Dorothy Sidney ("Sacharissa"), who married in 1639. When his plot to take over London for the king was discovered in 1643, he was heavily fined and exiled to France. In 1651 he was pardoned and went back to England, where he returned to Parliament after the Restoration. He died in 1687. In 1645 three unauthorized editions of his *Poems* appeared, which he disowned in the first authorized edition of 1664.

JOHN WILMOT, EARL OF ROCHESTER, born in 1647, inherited the earldom in 1658. He was educated at Wadham College, Oxford, and then made a tour of France and Italy. He became a leading figure among the wits surrounding Charles II, notorious for his debauchery, and was considered to be the original for Dorimant in Etheredge's *The Man of Mode*. But after a period of searching and doubt, he renounced his libertine attitudes and accepted religion before his death in 1680. A badly printed and dubiously selected edition of his *Poems* was printed in 1680, and another in 1685, but not until 1690/91 did a reliable selection appear, printed by Tonson and enlarged in 1713.

Henry King

Upon the Death of My Ever-Desired Friend Doctor Donne, Dean of Paul's

To have lived eminent in a degree
Beyond our loftiest flights, that is, like thee,
Or t' have had too much merit is not safe;
For such excesses find no epitaph.
At common graves we have poetic eyes
Can melt themselves in easy elegies;
Each quill can drop his tributary verse,
And pin it, with the hatchments, to the hearse.
But at thine, poem or inscriptiòn
(Rich soul of wit and language) we have none;   10
Indeed a silence does that tomb befit
Where is no herald left to blazon it.
Widowed invention justly doth forbear
To come abroad, knowing thou art not here,
Late her great patron; whose prerogative
Maintained and clothed her so, as none alive
Must now presume to keep her at thy rate,
Though he the Indies for her dower estate:
Or else that awful fire which once did burn
In thy clear brain, now fall'n into thy urn,   20
Lives there to fright rude empirics from thence,
Which might profane thee by their ignorance.
Whoever writes of thee, and in a style
Unworthy such a theme, does but revile
Thy precious dust, and wake a learned spirit
Which may revenge his rapes upon thy merit.
For all a low-pitched fancy can devise
Will prove at best but hallowed injuries.

Thou, like the dying swan, didst lately sing
Thy mournful dirge in audience of the King;   30
When pale looks and faint accents of thy breath
Presented so to life that piece of death,
That it was feared and prophesied by all

[*Upon the Death of . . . Doctor Donne . . .*]   25

Thou hither cam'st to preach thy funeral.
O! hadst thou in an elegiac knell
Rung out unto the world thine own farewell,
And in thy high victorious numbers beat
The solemn measure of thy grieved retreat,
Thou might'st the poet's service now have missed,   40
As well as then thou didst prevent the priest,
And never to the world beholden be
So much as for an epitaph for thee.

   I do not like the office. Nor is't fit
Thou, who didst lend our age such sums of wit,
Shouldst now reborrow from her bankrupt mine
That ore to bury thee which once was thine.
Rather, still leave us in thy debt; and know
(Exalted soul) more glory 'tis to owe
Unto thy hearse what we can never pay,
Than with embasèd coin those rites defray.   50

   Commit we then thee to thyself. Nor blame
Our drooping loves, which thus to thine own fame
Leave thee executor, since but by thy own
No pen could do thee justice, nor bays crown
Thy vast desert; save that, we nothing can
Depute to be thy ashes' guardian.

   So jewellers no art or metal trust
To form the diamond, but the diamond's dust.

The Exequy

Accept, thou shrine of my dead saint,
Instead of dirges this complaint;
And for sweet flowers to crown thy hearse,
Receive a strew of weeping verse
From thy grieved friend, whom thou might'st see
Quite melted into tears for thee.
Dear loss! since thy untimely fate
My task hath been to meditate

On thee, on thee: thou art the book,
The library whereon I look,   10
Though almost blind. For thee (loved clay)
I languish out, not live, the day,
Using no other exercise
But what I practise with mine eyes;
By which wet glasses I find out
How lazily time creeps about
To one that mourns; this, only this,
My exercise and business is.
So I compute the weary hours
With sighs dissolvèd into showers.   20

Nor wonder if my time go thus
Backward and most preposterous;
Thou hast benighted me; thy set
This eve of blackness did beget,
Who wast my day (though overcast
Before thou hadst thy noontide passed)
And I remember must in tears,
Thou scarce hadst seen so many years
As day tells hours. By thy clear sun
My love and fortune first did run;   30
But thou wilt never more appear
Folded within my hemisphere,
Since both thy light and motiòn
Like a fled star is fall'n and gone;
And 'twixt me and my soul's dear wish
An earth now interposèd is,
Which such a strange eclipse doth make
As ne'er was read in almanac.

I could allow thee for a time
To darken me and my sad clime;   40
Were it a month, a year, or ten,
I would thy exile live till then,
And all that space my mirth adjourn,
So thou wouldst promise to return,
And putting off thy ashy shroud,
At length disperse this sorrow's cloud.

But woe is me! the longest date
Too narrow is to calculate
These empty hopes; never shall I
Be so much blest as to descry   50
A glimpse of thee, till that day come
Which shall the earth to cinders doom,
And a fierce fever must calcine
The body of this world like thine,
(My little world). That fit of fire
Once off, our bodies shall aspire
To our souls' bliss; then we shall rise
And view ourselves with clearer eyes
In that calm region where no night
Can hide us from each other's sight.   60

Meantime, thou hast her, earth; much good
May my harm do thee. Since it stood
With Heaven's will I might not call
Her longer mine, I give thee all
My short-lived right and interest
In her whom living I loved best;
With a most free and bounteous grief,
I give thee what I could not keep.
Be kind to her, and prithee look
Thou write into thy doomsday book   70
Each parcel of this rarity
Which in thy casket shrined doth lie.
See that thou make thy reck'ning straight,
And yield her back again by weight;
For thou must audit on thy trust
Each grain and atom of this dust,
As thou wilt answer Him that lent,
Not gave thee, my dear monument.

So close the ground, and 'bout her shade
Black curtains draw; my bride is laid.   80

Sleep on, my love, in thy cold bed
Never to be disquieted!
My last good-night! Thou wilt not wake

[*Henry King*]   28

Till I thy fate shall overtake;
Till age, or grief, or sickness must
Marry my body to that dust
It so much loves; and fill the room
My heart keeps empty in thy tomb.
Stay for me there, I will not fail
To meet thee in that hollow vale. 90
And think not much of my delay;
I am already on the way,
And follow thee with all the speed
Desire can make, or sorrows breed.
Each minute is a short degree,
And ev'ry hour a step towards thee.
At night when I betake to rest,
Next morn I rise nearer my west
Of life, almost by eight hours' sail,
Than when sleep breathed his drowsy gale. 100

Thus from the sun my bottom steers,
And my day's compass downward bears;
Nor labor I to stem the tide
Through which to thee I swiftly glide.

'Tis true, with shame and grief I yield,
Thou like the van first took'st the field,
And gotten hath the victory
In thus adventuring to die
Before me, whose more years might crave
A just precedence in the grave. 110
But hark! my pulse like a soft drum
Beats my approach, tells thee I come;
And slow howe'er my marches be,
I shall at last sit down by thee.

The thought of this bids me go on,
And wait my dissolutiòn
With hope and comfort. Dear (forgive
The crime) I am content to live
Divided, with but half a heart,
Till we shall meet and never part. 120

[*The Exequy*] 29

To My Sister, Anne King,
Who Chid Me in Verse for Being Angry

Dear Nan! I would not have thy counsel lost,
Though I last night had twice so much been crossed;
Well is a passion to the market brought,
When such a treasure of advice is bought
With so much dross. And could'st thou me assure,
Each vice of mine should meet with such a cure,
I would sin oft, and on my guilty brow
Wear every misperfection that I owe,
Open and visible; I should not hide
But bring my faults abroad: to hear thee chide   10
In such a note, and with a quill so sage,
It passion tunes, and calms a tempest's rage.

    Well, I am charmed, and promise to redress
What, without shrift, my follies do confess
Against myself: wherefore let me entreat,
When I fly out in that distempered heat
Which frets me into fasts, thou wilt reprove
That froward spleen in poetry and love;
So though I lose my reason in such fits
Thou'lt rhyme me back again into my wits.   20

The Forlorn Hope

How long (vain Hope!) dost thou my joys suspend?
Say, must my expectation know no end?
Thou wast more kind unto the wand'ring Greek
Who did ten years his wife and country seek:
    Ten lazy winters in my glass are run,
    Yet my thought's travail seems but new begun.

Smooth quicksand which the easy world beguiles!
Thou shalt not bury me in thy false smiles.
They that in hunting shadows pleasure take,
May benefit of thy illusion make.   10

[Henry King] 30

Since thou hast banish'd me from my content
I here pronounce thy final banishment.

Farewell, thou dream of nothing! thou mere voice!
Get thee to fools that can feed fat with noise:
Bid wretches marked for death look for reprieve,
Or men broke on the wheel persuade to live.
    Henceforth my comfort and best hope shall be,
    By scorning Hope, ne'er to rely on thee.

Sic Vita

Like to the falling of a star;
Or as the flights of eagles are;
Or like the fresh spring's gaudy hue;
Or silver drops of morning dew;
Or like a wind that chafes the flood;
Or bubbles which on water stood;
Even such is man, whose borrowed light
Is straight called in, and paid to night.

    The wind blows out; the bubble dies;
    The spring entombed in autumn lies;
    The dew dries up; the star is shot;
    The flight is past; and man forgot.

A Contemplation Upon Flowers

Brave flowers, that I could gallant it like you
And be as little vain;
You come abroad, and make a harmless show,
And to your beds of earth again;
You are not proud, you know your birth
For your embroidered garments are from earth.

You do obey your months and times, but I
Would have it ever spring;
My fate would know no winter, never die

[*A Contemplation Upon Flowers*] 31

Nor think of such a thing;   10
Oh, that I could my bed of earth but view
And smile, and look as cheerfully as you.

Oh, teach me to see death and not to fear,
But rather to take truce;
How often have I seen you at a bier,
And there look fresh and spruce;
You fragrant flowers then teach me that my breath
Like yours may sweeten, and perfume my death.

Sonnet

Tell me no more how fair she is,
    I have no mind to hear
The story of that distant bliss
    I never shall come near;
By sad experience I have found
That her perfection is my wound.

And tell me not how fond I am
    To tempt a daring fate,
From whence no triumph ever came
    But to repent too late;   10
There is some hope ere long I may
In silence dote myself away.

I ask no pity (Love) from thee,
    Nor will thy justice blame,
So that thou wilt not envy me
    The glory of my flame,
Which crowns my heart whene'er it dies,
In that it falls her sacrifice.

The Change

    EL SABIO MUDA CONSCIO: EL LOCO PERSEVERA

We loved as friends now twenty years and more:

Is't time or reason, think you, to give o'er?
When, though two prenti'ships set Jacob free,
I have not held my Rachel dear at three.

Yet will I not your levity accuse;
Continuance sometimes is the worse abuse.
In judgement I might rather hold it strange,
If, like the fleeting world, you did not change:
Be it your wisdom therefore to retract,
When perseverance oft is folly's act.   10

In pity I can think, that what you do
Hath justice in't, and some religion too;
For of all virtues moral or divine,
We know, but love, none must in Heaven shine;
Well did you the presumption then foresee
Of counterfeiting immortality;
Since had you kept our loves too long alive,
We might invade Heaven's prerogative;
Or in our progress, like the Jews, comprise
The legend of an earthly Paradise.   20

Live happy, and more prosperous in the next.
You have discharg'd your old friend by the text.
Farewell, fair shadow of a female faith,
And let this be our friendship's epitaph:
Affection shares the frailty of our fate,
When (like ourselves) 'tis old and out of date;
'Tis just all human loves their period have,
When friends are frail and dropping to the grave.

The Retreat

Pursue no more (my thoughts!) that false unkind;
You may as soon imprison the north-wind,
Or catch the lightning as it leaps, or reach
The leading billow first ran down the breach,
Or undertake the flying clouds to track
In the same path they yesterday did rack.

     Then, like a torch turned downward, let the same
     Desire which nourished it, put out your flame.

Lo, thus I do divorce thee from my breast,
False to thy vow, and traitor to my rest!   10
Henceforth thy tears shall be (though thou repent)
Like pardons after execution sent.
Nor shalt thou ever my love's story read,
But as some epitaph of what is dead.
     So may my hope on future blessings dwell,
     As 'tis my firm resolve and last farewell.

The Surrender

My once dear love, hapless that I no more
Must call thee so, the rich affection's store
That fed our hopes lies now exhaust and spent,
Like sums of treasure unto bankrupts lent.

We that did nothing study but the way
To love each other, with which thoughts the day
Rose with delight to us, and with them set,
Must learn the hateful art how to forget.
We that did nothing wish that Heav'n could give
Beyond ourselves, nor did desire to live   10
Beyond that wish, all these now cancel must
As if not writ in faith, but words and dust.

Yet witness those clear vows which lovers make,
Witness the chaste desires that never brake
Into unruly heats; witness that breast
Which in thy bosom anchored his whole rest;
'Tis no default in us, I dare acquite
Thy maiden faith, thy purpose fair and white
As thy pure self. Cross planets did envy
Us to each other, and Heav'n did untie   20
Faster than vows could bind. Oh, that the stars,
When lovers meet, should stand opposed in wars!

Since, then, some higher destinies command,
Let us not strive, nor labor to withstand
What is past help. The longest date of grief
Can never yield a hope of our relief;
And though we waste ourselves in moist laments,
Tears may drown us, but not our discontents.

Fold back our arms, take home our fruitless loves,
That must new fortunes try, like turtledoves   30
Dislodgèd from their haunts. We must in tears
Unwind a love knit up in many years.
In this last kiss I here surrender thee
Back to thyself, so thou again art free;
Thou in another, sad as that, resend
The truest heart that lover e'er did lend.

Now turn from each. So fare our severed hearts
As the divorced soul from her body parts.

Thomas Carew

An Elegy Upon the Death of Doctor Donne, Dean of Paul's

Can we not force from widowed poetry,
Now thou art dead (great Donne) one elegy
To crown thy hearse? Why yet did we not trust,
Though with unkneaded dough-baked prose, thy dust,
Such as the unscissored churchman from the flower
Of fading rhet'ric, short-lived as his hour,
Dry as the sand that measures it, should lay
Upon the ashes, on the funeral day?
Have we no voice, nor tune? Didst thou dispense
Through all our language both the words and sense? 10
'Tis a sad truth. The pulpit may her plain
And sober Christian precepts still retain;
Doctrines it may, and wholesome uses, frame;
Grave homilies and lectures, but the flame
Of thy brave soul (that shot such heat and light
As burnt our earth, and made our darkness bright,
Committed holy rapes upon our will,
Did through the eye the melting heart distil,
And the deep knowledge of dark truths so teach
As sense might judge, what fancy could not reach) 20
Must be desired for ever. So the fire
That fills with spirit and heat the Delphic choir,
Which, kindled first by thy Promethean breath,
Glowed here a while, lies quenched now in thy death.
The Muses' garden with pedantic weeds
O'erspread, was purged by thee; the lazy seeds
Of servile imitation thrown away,
And fresh invention planted; thou didst pay
The debts of our penurious bankrupt age;
Licentious thefts, that make poetic rage   30
A mimic fury, when our souls must be
Possessed, or with Anacreon's ecstasy
Or Pindar's, not their own; the subtle cheat
Of sly exchanges, and the juggling feat

Of two-edged words, or whatsoever wrong
By ours was done the Greek or Latin tongue,
Thou hast redeemed, and opened us a mine
Of rich and pregnant fancy; drawn a line
Of masculine expression, which had good
Old Orpheus seen, or all the ancient brood   40
Our superstitious fools admire and hold
Their lead more precious than thy burnished gold,
Thou hadst been their exchequer, and no more
They each in other's dust had raked for ore.
Thou shalt yield no precedence, but of time
And the blind fate of language, whose tuned chime
More charms the outward sense; yet thou mayst claim
From so great disadvantage greater fame,
Since to the awe of thy imperious wit
Our stubborn language bends, made only fit   50
With her tough thick-ribbed hoops to gird about
Thy giant fancy, which had proved too stout
For their soft melting phrases. As in time
They had the start, so did they cull the prime
Buds of invention many a hundred year,
And left the rifled fields, besides the fear
To touch their harvest; yet from those bare lands
Of what is purely thine, thy only hands,
(And that their smallest work) have gleanèd more
Than all those times and tongues could reap before.   60
   But thou art gone, and thy strict laws will be
Too hard for libertines in poetry;
They will recall the goodly exiled train
Of gods and goddesses, which in thy just reign
Were banished nobler poems; now with these,
The silenced tales i' th' *Metamorphoses*,
Shall stuff their lines, and swell the windy page,
Till verse, refined by thee in this last age,
Turn ballad-rhyme, or those old idols be
Adored again with new apostasy.   70
   O, pardon me, that break with untuned verse
The reverend silence that attends thy hearse,
Whose awful solemn murmurs were to thee,
More than these faint lines, a loud elegy,

That did proclaim in a dumb eloquence
The death of all the arts; whose influence,
Grown feeble, in these panting numbers lies
Gasping short-winded accents, and so dies.
So doth the swiftly turning wheel not stand
In the instant we withdraw the moving hand,   80
But some small time retain a faint weak course,
By virtue of the first impulsive force;
And so, whilst I cast on thy funeral pile
The crown of bays, oh, let it crack awhile,
And spit disdain, till the devouring flashes
Suck all the moisture up, then turn to ashes.
    I will not draw thee envy to engross
All thy perfections, or weep all the loss;
Those are too numerous for an elegy,
And this too great to be expressed by me.   90
Though every pen should share a distinct part,
Yet art thou theme enough to tire all art;
Let others carve the rest, it shall suffice
I on thy tomb this epitaph incise.

    Here lies a king, that ruled as he thought fit
    The universal monarchy of wit;
    Here lie two flamens, and both those, the best,
    Apollo's first, at last, the true God's priest.

The Spring

Now that the winter's gone, the earth hath lost
Her snow-white robes, and now no more the frost
Candies the grass, or casts an icy cream
Upon the silver lake or crystal stream:
But the warm sun thaws the benumbèd earth,
And makes it tender; gives a sacred birth
To the dead swallow; wakes in hollow tree
The drowsy cuckoo and the humblebee.
Now do a choir of chirping minstrels bring,
In triumph to the world, the youthful spring.   10
The valleys, hills, and woods in rich array
                                        [*Thomas Carew*] 38

Welcome the coming of the longed-for May.
Now all things smile; only my love doth lour;
Nor hath the scalding noonday sun the power
To melt that marble ice, which still doth hold
Her heart congealed, and makes her pity cold.
The ox which lately did for shelter fly
Into the stall, doth now securely lie
In open fields; and love no more is made
By the fireside; but in the cooler shade   20
Amyntas now doth with his Chloris sleep
Under a sycamore, and all things keep
Time with the season: only she doth carry
June in her eyes, in her heart January.

Ingrateful Beauty Threatened

Know, Celia (since thou art so proud),
  'Twas I that gave thee thy renown;
Thou hadst, in the forgotten crowd
  Of common beauties, lived unknown,
Had not my verse exhaled thy name,
And with it imped the wings of fame.

That killing power is none of thine,
  I gave it to thy voice and eyes;
Thy sweets, thy graces, all are mine;
  Thou art my star, shin'st in my skies;   10
Then dart not from thy borrowed sphere
Lightning on him that fixed thee there.

Tempt me with such affrights no more,
  Lest what I made I uncreate;
Let fools thy mystic forms adore,
  I'll know thee in thy mortal state;
Wise poets that wrapped truth in tales
Knew her themselves through all her veils.

In Answer of an Elegiacal Letter

From Aurelian Townshend,
inviting me to write on that subject

Why dost thou sound, my dear Aurelian,
In so shrill accents from the Barbican,
A loud alarum to my drowsy eyes,
Bidding them wake in tears and elegies
For mighty Sweden's fall? Alas! how may
My lyric feet, that of the smooth soft way
Of love and beauty only know the tread,
In dancing paces celebrate the dead
Victorious king, or his majestic hearse
Profane with th' humble touch of their low verse?   10
Virgil, nor Lucan, no, nor Tasso, more
Than both, not Donne, worth all that went before,
With the united labor of their wit,
Could a just poem to this subject fit.
His actions were too mighty to be raised
Higher by verse; let him in prose be praised,
In modest faithful story, which his deeds
Shall turn to poems. When the next age reads
Of Frankfort, Leipzig, Wurzburg, of the Rhine,
The Lech, the Danube, Tilly, Wallenstein,   20
Bavaria, Pappenhaim, Lutzen-field, where he
Gained after death a posthume victory,
They'll think his acts things rather feigned than done,
Like our romances of The Knight o' the Sun.
Leave we him, then, to the grave chronicler,
Who, though to annals he cannot refer
His too-brief story, yet his journals may
Stand by the Caesars' years, and, every day
Cut into minutes, each shall more contain
Of great designment than an emperor's reign.   30
And (since 'twas but his churchyard) let him have
For his own ashes now no narrower grave
Than the whole German continent's vast womb,
Whilst all her cities do but make his tomb.

[Thomas Carew]   40

Let us to supreme Providence commit
The fate of monarchs, which first thought it fit
To rend the empire from the Austrian grasp,
And next from Sweden's, even when he did clasp
Within his dying arms the sovereignty
Of all those provinces, that men might see   40
The divine wisdom would not leave that land
Subject to any one king's sole command.
Then let the Germans fear if Caesar shall,
Or the United Princes, rise and fall;
But let us, that in myrtle bowers sit
Under secure shades, use the benefit
Of peace and plenty, which the blessed hand
Of our good king gives this obdurate land;
Let us of revels sing, and let thy breath,
(Which filled fame's trumpet with Gustavus' death,   50
Blowing his name to heaven) gently inspire
Thy past'ral pipe, till all our swains admire
Thy song and subject, whilst they both comprise
The beauties of the *Shepherd's Paradise*.
For who like thee (whose loose discourse is far
More neat and polished than our poems are,
Whose very gait's more graceful than our dance)
In sweetly-flowing numbers may advance
The glorious night? When, not to act foul rapes,
Like birds or beasts, but in their angel-shapes   60
A troop of deities came down to guide
Our steerless barks in passion's swelling tide
By virtue's card, and brought us from above
A pattern of their own celestial love.
Nor lay it in dark sullen precepts drowned,
But with rich fancy and clear action crowned
Through a mysterious fable (that was drawn,
Like a transparent veil of purest lawn,
Before their dazzling beauties) the divine
Venus did with her heavenly Cupid shine.   70
The story's curious web, the masculine style,
The subtle sense, did time and sleep beguile;
Pinioned and charmed they stood to gaze upon
Th' angelic forms, gestures and motion;

To hear those ravishing sounds that did dispense
Knowledge and pleasure to the soul and sense.
It fill'd us with amazement to behold
Love made all spirit; his corporeal mould,
Dissected into atoms, melt away
To empty air, and from the gross allay   80
Of mixtures and compounding accidents
Refined to immaterial elements.
But when the Queen of Beauty did inspire
The air with perfumes, and our hearts with fire,
Breathing from her celestial organ sweet
Harmonious notes, our souls fell at her feet,
And did with humble reverend duty more
Her rare perfections than high state adore.
    These harmless pastimes let my Townshend sing
To rural tunes; not that thy Muse wants wing   90
To soar a loftier pitch, for she hath made
A noble flight, and placed th' heroic shade
Above the reach of our faint flagging rhyme;
But these are subjects proper to our clime,
Tourneys, masques, theatres, better become
Our halcyon days. What though the German drum
Bellow for freedom and revenge, the noise
Concerns not us, nor should divert our joys;
Nor ought the thunder of their carabins
Drown the sweet airs of our tuned violins.   100
Believe me, friend, if their prevailing powers
Gain them a calm security like ours,
They'll hang their arms up on the olive bough,
And dance and revel then, as we do now.

A Prayer to the Wind

Go, thou gentle whispering wind,
Bear this sigh, and if thou find
Where my cruel fair doth rest,
Cast it in her snowy breast;
So, inflamed by my desire,
It may set her heart afire.

                          [Thomas Carew]   42

Those sweet kisses thou shalt gain
Will reward thee for thy pain.
Boldly light upon her lip,
There suck odors, and thence skip   10
To her bosom; lastly fall
Down, and wander over all.
Range about those ivory hills,
From whose every part distils
Amber dew; there spices grow,
There pure streams of nectar flow;
There perfume thyself, and bring
All those sweets upon thy wing.
As thou return'st, change by thy power
Every weed into a flower;   20
Turn each thistle to a vine,
Make the bramble eglantine;
For so rich a booty made,
Do but this, and I am paid.
Thou canst with thy powerful blast
Heat apace, and cool as fast;
Thou canst kindle hidden flame,
And again destroy the same;
Then, for pity, either stir
Up the fire of love in her,   30
That alike both flames may shine,
Or else quite extinguish mine.

Mediocrity in Love Rejected

Give me more love, or more disdain:
   The torrid, or the frozen zone
Bring equal ease unto my pain,
   The temperate affords me none;
Either extreme, of love or hate,
Is sweeter than a calm estate.
Give me a storm; if it be love,
   Like Danaë in that golden shower,
I swim in pleasure; if it prove
   Disdain, that torrent will devour   10

My vulture-hopes; and he's possessed
Of heaven, that's but from hell released
    Then crown my joys, or cure my pain:
    Give me more love or more disdain.

To My Worthy Friend, Master George Sandys, On His Translation of the Psalms

I press not to the choir, nor dare I greet
The holy place with my unhallowed feet;
My unwashed muse pollutes not things divine,
Nor mingles her profaner notes with thine;
Here humbly at the porch she stays,
And with glad ears sucks in thy sacred lays.
So devout penitents of old were wont,
Some without door, and some beneath the font,
To stand and hear the Church's liturgies,
Yet not assist the solemn exercise.   10
Sufficeth her that she a lay-place gain,
To trim thy vestments, or but bear thy train;
Though not in tune or wing she reach thy lark,
Her lyric feet may dance before the Ark.
Who knows but that her wand'ring eyes that run
Now hunting glowworms, may adore the sun?
A pure flame may, shot by almighty power
Into her breast, the earthly flame devour.
My eyes in penitential dew may steep
That brine, which they for sensual love did weep.   20
So (though 'gainst nature's course) fire may be quenched
With fire, and water be with water drenched.
Perhaps my restless soul, tired with pursuit
Of mortal beauty, seeking without fruit
Contentment there, which hath not, when enjoyed,
Quenched all her thirst, nor satisfied though cloyed,
Weary of her vain search below, above
In the first fair may find th' immortal love.
Prompted by thy example then, no more
In molds of clay will I my God adore;   30
But tear those idols from my heart, and write
What His blest sp'rit, not fond love, shall indite.

                   [Thomas Carew] 44

Then I no more shall court the verdant bay,
But the dry leafless trunk on Golgothà;
And rather strive to gain from thence one thorn,
Than all the flourishing wreaths by laureates worn.

A Song

Ask me no more where Jove bestows,
When June is past, the fading rose;
For in your beauty's orient deep
These flowers as in their causes, sleep.

Ask me no more whither doth stray
The golden atoms of the day;
For in pure love heaven did prepare
Those powders to enrich your hair.

Ask me no more whither doth haste
The nightingale, when May is past;   10
For in your sweet dividing throat
She winters and keeps warm her note.

Ask me no more where those stars light,
That downwards fall in dead of night;
For in your eyes they sit, and there,
Fixèd become, as in their sphere.

Ask me no more if east or west
The phoenix builds her spicy nest;
For unto you at last she flies,
And in your fragrant bosom dies.   20

Love's Force

In the first ruder age, when love was wild,
Not yet by laws reclaimed, not reconciled
To order, nor by reason manned, but flew
Full-summed by nature, on the instant view

[*Love's Force*] 45

Upon the wings of appetite, at all
The eye could fair, or sense delightful call;
Election was not yet, but as their cheap
Food from the oak, or the next acorn-heap,
As water from the nearest spring or brook,
So men their undistinguish'd females took   10
By chance, not choice; but soon the heavenly spark
That in man's bosom lurked, broke through this dark
Confusion: then the noblest breast first felt
Itself for its own proper object melt.

Eternity of Love Protested

How ill doth he deserve a lover's name,
            Whose pale weak flame
            Cannot retain
His heat in spite of absence or disdain;
But doth at once, like paper set on fire,
            Burn and expire!
True love can never change his seat,
Nor did he ever love that could retreat.

That noble flame, which my breast keeps alive,
            Shall still survive,   10
            When my soul's fled;
Nor shall my love die when my body's dead,
That shall wait on me to the lower shade,
            And never fade;
My very ashes in their urn
Shall like a hallowed lamp for ever burn.

To Ben Jonson

*Upon occasion of his ode of defiance
annexed to his play of The New Inn*

'Tis true (dear Ben) thy just chastising hand
Hath fixed upon the sotted age a brand
To their swollen pride and empty scribbling due;

[*Thomas Carew*] 46

It can nor judge, nor write, and yet 'tis true
Thy comic muse, from the exalted line
Touched by thy *Alchemist*, doth since decline
From that her zenith, and foretells a red
And blushing evening, when she goes to bed,
Yet such as shall outshine the glimmering light
With which all stars shall gild the following night.   10
Nor think it much (since all thy eaglets may
Endure the sunny trial) if we say
This hath the stronger wing, or that doth shine
Tricked up in fairer plumes, since all are thine.
Who hath his flock of cackling geese compared
With thy tuned choir of swans? or else who dared
To call thy births deformed? But if thou bind
By city-custom, or by gavelkind,
In equal shares thy love on all thy race,
We may distinguish of their sex and place;   20
Though one hand form them, and though one brain strike
Souls into all, they are not all alike.
Why should the follies, then, of this dull age
Draw from thy pen such an immodest rage
As seems to blast thy (else immortal) bays,
When thine own tongue proclaims thy itch of praise?
Such thirst will argue drought. No, let be hurled
Upon thy works by the detracting world
What malice can suggest; let the rout say,
The running sands, that (ere thou make a play)   30
Count the slow minutes, might a Goodwin frame
To swallow, when th' hast done, thy shipwrecked name.
Let them the dear expense of oil upbraid,
Sucked by thy watchful lamp, that hath betrayed
To theft the blood of martyred authors, spilt
Into thy ink, whilst thou growest pale with guilt.
Repine not at the taper's thrifty waste,
That sleeks thy terser poems; nor is haste
Praise, but excuse; and if thou overcome
A knotty writer, bring the booty home;   40
Nor think it theft if the rich spoils so torn
From conquered authors be as trophies worn.
Let others glut on the extorted praise

Of vulgar breath; trust thou to after-days.
Thy labored works shall live when time devours
Th' abortive offspring of their hasty hours.
Thou art not of their rank, the quarrel lies
Within thine own verge; then let this suffice,
The wiser world doth greater thee confess
Than all men else, than thyself only less.   50

To My Inconstant Mistress

When thou, poor excommunicate
  From all the joys of love, shalt see
The full reward and glorious fate
  Which my strong faith shall purchase me,
  Then curse thine own inconstancy.

A fairer hand than thine shall cure
  That heart which thy false oaths did wound;
And to my soul, a soul more pure
  Than thine shall by love's hand be bound,
  And both with equal glory crowned.   10

Then shalt thou weep, entreat, complain
  To love, as I did once to thee;
When all thy tears shall be as vain
  As mine were then, for thou shalt be
  Damned for thy false apostasy.

Upon a Ribbon

This silken wreath, which circles in mine arm,
Is but an emblem of that mystic charm
Wherewith the magic of your beauties binds
My captive soul, and round about it winds
Fetters of lasting love. This hath entwined
My flesh alone; that hath empaled my mind.
Time may wear out these soft weak bands, but those
Strong chains of brass, fate shall not discompose.

[Thomas Carew] 48

This holy relic may preserve my wrist,
But my whole frame doth by that power subsist;   10
To that my prayers and sacrifice, to this
I only pay a superstitious kiss.
This but the idol, that's the deity;
Religion there is due; here, ceremony.
That I receive by faith, this but in trust;
Here I may tender duty, there I must.
This order as a layman I may bear,
But I become Love's priest when that I wear;
This moves like air; that as the center stands;
That knot your virtue tied, this but your hands;   20
That, nature framed; but this was made by art;
This makes my arm your prisoner; that my heart.

To a Lady that Desired I Would Love Her

Now you have freely given me leave to love,
        What will you do?
Shall I your mirth or passion move
        When I begin to woo?
Will you torment, or scorn, or love me too?

Each petty beauty can disdain, and I,
        Spite of your hate,
Without your leave can see, and die;
        Dispense a nobler fate:
'Tis easy to destroy, you may create.   10

Then give me leave to love, and love me too,
        Not with design
To raise, as love's curst rebels do
        When puling poets whine,
Fame to their beauty, from their blubbered eyne.

Grief is a puddle, and reflects not clear
        Your beauty's rays;
Joys are pure streams, your eyes appear
        Sullen in sadder lays;
In cheerful numbers they shine bright with praise,   20

Which shall not mention, to express you fair,
       Wounds, flames, and darts,
Storms in your brow, nets in your hair,
       Suborning all your parts,
Or to betray or torture captive hearts.

I'll make your eyes like morning suns appear,
       As mild and fair,
Your brow as crystal, smooth and clear,
       And your dishevelled hair
Shall flow like a calm region of the air.   30

Rich nature's store, which is the poet's treasure,
       I'll spend to dress
Your beauties, if your mine of pleasure
       In equal thankfulness
You but unlock, so we each other bless.

Epitaph on the Lady Mary Villiers

This little vault, this narrow room,
Of love and beauty is the tomb;
The dawning beam that 'gan to clear
Our clouded sky, lies darkened here,
Forever set to us, by death
Sent to inflame the world beneath.
'Twas but a bud, yet did contain
More sweetness than shall spring again;
A budding star that might have grown
Into a sun, when it had blown.   10
This hopeful beauty did create
New life in love's declining state;
But now his empire ends, and we
From fire and wounding darts are free;
His brand, his bow, let no man fear—
The flames, the arrows, all lie here.

Boldness in Love

Mark how the bashful morn in vain
Courts the amorous marigold,
With sighing blasts and weeping rain,
Yet she refuses to unfold.
But when the planet of the day
Approacheth with his powerful ray,
Then she spreads, then she receives
His warmer beams into her virgin leaves.
So shalt thou thrive in love, fond boy:
If thy tears and sighs discover   10
Thy grief, thou never shalt enjoy
The just reward of a bold lover;
But when with moving accents thou
Shalt constant faith and service vow,
Thy Celia shall receive those charms
With open ears, and with unfolded arms.

Sir John Suckling

Upon My Lady Carlisle's Walking in Hampton Court Garden

Dialogue

T[homas] C[arew]   J[ohn] S[uckling]

Tom. Didst thou not find the place inspired,
       And flowers, as if they had desired
       No other sun, start from their beds,
       And for a sight steal out their heads?
       Heard'st thou not music when she talked?
       And didst not find that, as she walked
       She threw rare perfumes all about,
       Such as bean-blossoms newly out,
       Or chafed spices give?—

J. S. I must confess those perfumes, Tom,   10
       I did not smell; nor found that from
       Her passing by aught sprung up new:
       The flow'rs had all their birth from you;
       For I passed o'er the selfsame walk,
       And did not find one single stalk
       Of any thing that was to bring
       This unknown after-after-spring.

Tom. Dull and insensible, couldst see
       A thing so near a deity
       Move up and down, and feel no change?   20

J. S. None and so great were alike strange.
       I had my thoughts, but not your way;
       All are not born, sir, to the bay;
       Alas! Tom, I am flesh and blood,
       And was consulting how I could
       In spite of masks and hoods descry

The parts denied unto the eye:
I was undoing all she wore;
And had she walked but one turn more,
Eve in her first state had not been   30
More naked, or more plainly seen.

Tom. 'Twas well for thee she left the place;
There is great danger in that face;
But hadst thou viewed her leg and thigh,
And, upon that discovery,
Searched after parts that are more dear
(As fancy seldom stops so near),
No time or age had ever seen
So lost a thing as thou hadst been.

Song

I prithee send me back my heart,
  Since I cannot have thine;
For if from yours you will not part,
  Why then shouldst thou have mine?

Yet now I think on't, let it lie,
  To find it were in vain;
For th' hast a thief in either eye
  Would steal it back again.

Why should two hearts in one breast lie,
  And yet not lodge together?   10
O love, where is thy sympathy,
  If thus our breasts thou sever?

But love is such a mystery
  I cannot find it out;
For when I think I'm best resolved,
  I then am most in doubt.

Then farewell care, and farewell woe,
  I will no longer pine;

For I'll believe I have her heart
  As much as she hath mine.   **20**

A Ballad Upon a Wedding

I tell thee, Dick, where I have been,
Where I the rarest things have seen,
  Oh, things without compare!
Such sights again cannot be found
In any place on English ground,
  Be it at wake or fair.

At Charing Cross, hard by the way
Where we (thou know'st) do sell our hay,
  There is a house with stairs;
And there I did see coming down   **10**
Such folk as are not in our town,
  Vorty at least, in pairs.

Amongst the rest, one pestilent fine
(His beard no bigger, though, than thine)
  Walked on before the rest.
Our landlord looks like nothing to him;
The King (God bless him!), 'twould undo him
  Should he go still so dressed.

At course-a-park, without all doubt,
He should have been the first taken out   **20**
  By all the maids i' the town,
Though lusty Roger there had been,
Or little George upon the Green,
  Or Vincent of the Crown.

But wot you what? the youth was going
To make an end of all his wooing;
  The parson for him stayed.
Yet by his leave (for all his haste)
He did not so much wish all past,
  (Perchance) as did the maid.   **30**

The maid—and thereby hangs a tale;
For such a maid no Whitsun-ale
   Could ever yet produce;
No grape, that's kindly ripe, could be
So round, so plump, so soft as she,
   Nor half so full of juice.

Her finger was so small, the ring
Would not stay on, which they did bring;
   It was too wide a peck:
And to say truth (for out it must),   40
It looked like the great collar (just)
   About our young colt's neck.

Her feet beneath her petticoat,
Like little mice stole in and out,
   As if they feared the light;
But oh, she dances such a way!
No sun upon an Easter day
   Is half so fine a sight.

He would have kissed her once or twice,
But she would not, she was so nice,   50
   She would not do't in sight;
And then she looked as who should say,
"I will do what I list today,
   And you shall do't at night."

Her cheeks so rare a white was on,
No daisy makes comparison
   (Who sees them is undone);
For streaks of red were mingled there,
Such as are on a Katherne pear
   (The side that's next the sun).   60

Her lips were red, and one was thin,
Compared to that was next her chin
   (Some bee had stung it newly);
But, Dick, her eyes so guard her face

I durst no more upon them gaze
    Than on the sun in July.

Her mouth so small, when she does speak,
Thou'dst swear her teeth her words did break,
    That they might passage get;
But she so handled still the matter,   70
They came as good as ours, or better,
    And are not spent a whit.

If wishing should be any sin,
The parson himself had guilty been
    (She looked that day so purely);
And, did the youth so oft the feat
At night, as some did in conceit,
    It would have spoiled him surely.

Passion o' me, how I run on!
There's that that would be thought upon,   80
    I trow, besides the bride.
The business of the kitchen's great,
For it is fit that man should eat,
    Nor was it there denied.

Just in the nick the cook knocked thrice,
And all the waiters in a trice
    His summons did obey;
Each serving-man, with dish in hand,
Marched boldly up, like our trained band,
    Presented, and away.   90

When all the meat was on the table,
What man of knife or teeth was able
    To stay to be entreated?
And this the very reason was—
Before the parson could say grace,
    The company was seated.

Now hats fly off, and youths carouse;
Healths first go round, and then the house;

            [*Sir John Suckling*]   56

The bride's came thick and thick:
And when 'twas named another's health,   100
Perhaps he made it hers by stealth;
   (And who could help it, Dick?)

O' the sudden up they rise and dance;
Then sit again and sigh and glance;
   Then dance again and kiss;
Thus several ways the time did pass,
Whilst every woman wished her place,
   And every man wished his!

By this time all were stolen aside
To counsel and undress the bride,   110
   But that he must not know;
But yet 'twas thought he guessed her mind,
And did not mean to stay behind
   Above an hour or so.

When in he came, Dick, there she lay
Like new-fall'n snow melting away
   ('Twas time, I trow, to part);
Kisses were now the only stay,
Which soon she gave, as who would say,
   "God be with ye, with all my heart."   120

But just as heavens would have, to cross it,
In came the bridesmaids with the posset.
   The bridegroom eat in spite,
For, had he left the women to't,
It would have cost two hours to do't,
   Which were too much that night.

At length the candle's out; and now
All that they had not done, they do.
   What that is, who can tell?
But I believe it was no more   130
Than thou and I have done before
   With Bridget and with Nell.

Song

No, no, fair heretic, it needs must be
    But an ill love in me,
    And worse for thee.
For were it in my power
To love thee now this hour
    More than I did the last,
'Twould then so fall
    I might not love at all.
Love that can flow, and can admit increase,
Admits as well an ebb, and may grow less.   10

True love is still the same; the torrid zones,
    And those more frigid ones,
    It must not know;
For love, grown cold or hot,
Is lust or friendship, not
    The thing we have;
For that's a flame would die,
    Held down or up too high.
Then think I love more than I can express,
And would love more, could I but love thee less.   20

A Song to a Lute

Hast thou seen the down i' the air,
    When wanton blasts have tossed it?
Or the ship on the sea,
    When ruder waves have crossed it?
Hast thou marked the crocodile's weeping,
    Or the fox's sleeping?
Or hast viewed the peacock in his pride,
    Or the dove by his bride,
    When he courts for his lechery?
O, so fickle, O, so vain, O, so false, so false is she!

Sonnet I

Dost see how unregarded now
   That piece of beauty passes?
There was a time when I did vow
     To that alone;
  But mark the fate of faces,
That red and white works now no more on me
Than if it could not charm, or I not see.

And yet the face continues good,
   And I have still desires,
Am still the selfsame flesh and blood,   10
     As apt to melt
  And suffer from those fires;
Oh! some kind power unriddle where it lies,
Whether my heart be faulty, or her eyes?

She every day her man does kill,
   And I as often die;
Neither her power, then, nor my will
     Can questioned be.
   What is the mystery?
Sure beauty's empires, like to greater states,   20
Have certain periods set, and hidden fates.

Sonnet II

Of thee, kind boy, I ask no red and white,
    To make up my delight;
    No odd becoming graces,
Black eyes, or little know-not-whats in faces;
Make me but mad enough, give me good store
Of love for her I court;
    I ask no more,
'Tis love in love that makes the sport.

[Sonnet II]   59

There's no such thing as that we beauty call,
    It is mere cozenage all;   10
        For though some long ago,
Liked certain colors mingled so and so,
That doth not tie me now from choosing new,
If I a fancy take
    To black and blue,
That fancy doth it beauty make.

'Tis not the meat, but 'tis the appetite
    Makes eating a delight,
        And if I like one dish
More than another, that a pheasant is;   20
What in our watches, that in us is found,
So to the height and nick
    We up be wound,
No matter by what hand or trick.

Sonnet IIII

O! for some honest lover's ghost,
    Some kind unbodied post
        Sent from the shades below!
        I strangely long to know
Whether the nobler chaplets wear,
Those that their mistress' scorn did bear,
        Or those that were used kindly.

For whatsoe'er they tell us here
    To make those sufferings dear,
        'Twill there I fear, be found
        That to the being crowned   10
T' have loved alone will not suffice,
Unless we also have been wise,
        And have our loves enjoyed.

What posture can we think him in,
    That here unloved again
        Departs, and 's thither gone

                                    [*Sir John Suckling*]   60

Where each sits by his own?
Or how can that Elysium be,
Where I my mistress still must see   20
    Circled in others' arms?

For there the judges all are just,
    And Sophonisba must
    Be his whom she held dear,
    Not his who loved her here;
The sweet Philoclea, since she died,
Lies by her Pyrocles his side,
    Not by Amphialus.

Some bays, perchance, or myrtle bough,
    For difference crowns the brow   30
    Of those kind souls that were
    The noble martyrs here;
And if that be the only odds
(As who can tell?), ye kinder gods,
    Give me the woman here.

" 'Tis now since I sat down before"

'Tis now since I sat down before
    That foolish fort, a heart,
(Time strangely spent), a year and more,
    And still I did my part:

Made my approaches, from her hand
    Unto her lip did rise,
And did already understand
    The language of her eyes;

Proceeded on with no less art—
    My tongue was engineer;   10
I thought to undermine the heart
    By whispering in the ear.

When this did nothing, I brought down

Great cannon-oaths, and shot
A thousand thousand to the town;
   And still it yielded not.

I then resolved to starve the place
   By cutting off all kisses,
Praising and gazing on her face,
   And all such little blisses.   20

To draw her out, and from her strength,
   I drew all batteries in,
And brought myself to lie at length,
   As if no siege had been.

When I had done what man could do,
   And thought the place mine own,
The enemy lay quiet too,
   And smiled at all was done.

I sent to know from whence and where
   These hopes and this relief?   30
A spy informed, Honor was there,
   And did command in chief.

"March, march," quoth I; "the word straight give;
   Let's lose no time, but leave her;
That giant upon air will live,
   And hold it out for ever.

"To such a place our camp remove
   As will no siege abide;
I hate a fool that starves her love,
   Only to feed her pride."   40

"Out upon it! I have loved"

Out upon it! I have loved
   Three whole days together;
And am like to love three more,

[*Sir John Suckling*]   62

If it prove fair weather.

Time shall moult away his wings,
  Ere he shall discover
In the whole wide world again
  Such a constant lover.

But the spite on't is, no praise
  Is due at all to me: 10
Love with me had made no stays
  Had it any been but she.

Had it any been but she,
  And that very face,
There had been at least ere this
  A dozen dozen in her place.

Song

Why so pale and wan, fond lover?
  Prithee, why so pale?
Will, when looking well can't move her,
  Looking ill prevail?
  Prithee, why so pale?

Why so dull and mute, young sinner?
  Prithee, why so mute?
Will, when speaking well can't win her,
  Saying nothing do't?
  Prithee, why so mute?   10

Quit, quit, for shame; this will not move,
  This cannot take her.
If of herself she will not love,
  Nothing can make her:
  The devil take her!

Richard Lovelace

To Althea, from Prison

SONG

When Love with unconfinèd wings
   Hovers within my gates,
And my divine Althea brings
   To whisper at the grates;
When I lie tangled in her hair
   And fettered to her eye,
The gods that wanton in the air
   Know no such liberty.

When flowing cups run swiftly round,
   With no allaying Thames,   10
Our careless heads with roses bound,
   Our hearts with loyal flames;
When thirsty grief in wine we steep,
   When healths and draughts go free,
Fishes that tipple in the deep
   Know no such liberty.

When (like committed linnets) I
   With shriller throat shall sing
The sweetness, mercy, majesty,
   And glories of my King;   20
When I shall voice aloud how good
   He is, how great should be,
Enlargèd winds that curl the flood
   Know no such liberty.

Stone walls do not a prison make,
   Nor iron bars a cage:
Minds innocent and quiet take
   That for an hermitage.
If I have freedom in my love,
   And in my soul am free,   30

Angels alone, that soar above,
  Enjoy such liberty.

To Amarantha,
That She Would Dishevel Her Hair

SONG

  Amarantha sweet and fair,
Ah, braid no more that shining hair!
  As my curious hand or eye,
Hovering round thee let it fly.

  Let it fly as unconfined
As its calm ravisher, the wind,
  Who hath left his darling, th' East,
To wanton o'er that spicy nest.

  Ev'ry tress must be confessed
But neatly tangled at the best,   10
  Like a clue of golden thread,
Most excellently ravellèd.

  Do not then wind up that light
In ribands, and o'ercloud in night;
  Like the sun in's early ray,
But shake your head and scatter day.

  See, 'tis broke! Within this grove,
The bower, and the walks of love,
  Weary lie we down and rest,
And fan each other's panting breast.   20

  Here we'll strip and cool our fire
In cream below, in milk-baths higher;
  And when all wells are drawen dry,
I'll drink a tear out of thine eye.

  Which our very joys shall leave,
That sorrows thus we can deceive;

Or our very sorrows weep,
That joys so ripe, so little keep.

The Snail

Wise emblem of our politic world,
Sage snail, within thine own self curled,
Instruct me softly to make haste,
Whilst these my feet go slowly fast.
　　Compendious snail! thou seem'st to me
Large Euclid's strict epitome;
And in each diagram, dost fling
Thee from the point unto the ring.
A figure now triangular,
An oval now, and now a square;　　　　　　　IO
And then a serpentine dost crawl,
Now a straight line, now crook'd, now all.
　　Preventing rival of the day,
Th' art up and openest thy ray,
And ere the morn cradles the moon,
Th' art broke into a beauteous noon.
Then, when the sun sups in the deep,
Thy silver horns ere Cynthia's peep,
And thou, from thine own liquid bed,
New Phoebus, heav'st thy pleasant head.　　20
　　Who shall a name for thee create,
Deep riddle of mysterious state?
Bold nature, that gives common birth
To all products of sea and earth,
Of thee, as earthquakes, is afraid,
Nor will thy dire deliv'ry aid.
　　Thou thine own daughter, then, and sire,
That son and mother art entire,
That big still with thy self dost go,
And liv'st an aged embryo;　　　　　　　　30
That like the cubs of India,
Thou from thy self a while dost play;
But frighted with a dog or gun,
In thine own belly thou dost run,

[*Richard Lovelace*]　66

And as thy house was thine own womb,
So thine own womb concludes thy tomb.
　　But now I must (analys'd king)
Thy economic virtues sing;
Thou great staid husband still within,
Thou thee, that's thine, dost discipline;　　　　　40
And when thou art to progress bent,
Thou mov'st thy self and tenement,
As warlike Scythians travelled, you
Remove your men and city too;
Then, after a sad dearth and rain,
Thou scatterest thy silver train;
And when the trees grow nak'd and old,
Thou clothest them with cloth of gold,
Which from thy bowels thou dost spin,
And draw from the rich mines within.　　　　　50
　　Now hast thou changed thee saint, and made
Thy self a fane that's cupola'd;
And in thy wreathed cloister thou
Walkest thine own gray friar too;
Strict, and locked up, th' art hood all o'er,
And ne'er eliminat'st thy door.
On salads thou dost feed severe,
And 'stead of beads thou dropp'st a tear,
And when to rest each calls the bell,
Thou sleep'st within thy marble cell;　　　　　60
Where, in dark contemplation placed,
The sweets of nature thou dost taste;
Who now with time thy days resolve,
And in a jelly thee dissolve,
Like a shot star, which doth repair
Upward, and rarify the air.

Gratiana Dancing and Singing

See! with what constant motiòn,
Even and glorious as the sun,
　　Gratiana steers that noble frame,
Soft as her breast, sweet as her voice

That gave each winding law and poise,
　　And swifter than the wings of fame.

She beat the happy pavement
By such a star made firmament,
　　Which now no more the roof envies,
But swells up high with Atlas ev'n,　　　　　　　10
Bearing the brighter, nobler heav'n,
　　And in her, all the deities.

Each step trod out a lover's thought
And the ambitious hopes he brought,
　　Chained to her brave feet with such arts,
Such sweet command and gentle awe,
As when she ceased, we sighing saw
　　The floor lay paved with broken hearts.

So did she move; so did she sing
Like the harmonious spheres that bring　　　　20
　　Unto their rounds their music's aid;
Which she performèd such a way
As all th' enamored world will say
　　The Graces dancèd, and Apollo played.

The Grasshopper

　　To my noble friend, Mr. Charles Cotton

　　ODE

O thou that swing'st upon the waving hair
　　Of some well-fillèd oaten beard,
Drunk ev'ry night with a delicious tear
　　Dropped thee from heav'n, where now th'art reared.

The joys of earth and air are thine entire,
　　That with thy feet and wings dost hop and fly;
And, when thy poppy works, thou dost retire
　　To thy carved acorn-bed to lie.

　　　　　　　　　　　　[*Richard Lovelace*]　68

Up with the day, the sun thou welcom'st then,
  Sport'st in the gilt plats of his beams,   10
And all these merry days mak'st merry, men,
  Thyself, and melancholy streams.

But ah, the sickle! Golden ears are cropped;
  Ceres and Bacchus bid good night;
Sharp frosty fingers all your flowers have topped,
  And what scythes spared, winds shave off quite.

Poor verdant fool! and now green ice! thy joys
  Large and as lasting as thy perch of grass,
Bid us lay in 'gainst winter, rain, and poise
  Their floods with an o'erflowing glass.   20

Thou best of men and friends! we will create
  A genuine summer in each other's breast,
And spite of this cold time and frozen fate,
  Thaw us a warm seat to our rest.

Our sacred hearths shall burn eternally
  As vestal flames; the North Wind, he
Shall strike his frost-stretched wings, dissolve, and fly
  This Ætna in epitome.

Dropping December shall come weeping in,
  Bewail th' usurping of his reign;   30
But when in show'rs of old Greek we begin,
  Shall cry he hath his crown again.

Night as clear Hesper shall our tapers whip
  From the light casements where we play,
And the dark hag from her black mantle strip,
  And stick there everlasting day.

Thus richer than untempted kings are we,
  That asking nothing, nothing need:
Though lord of all what seas embrace, yet he
  That wants himself is poor indeed.   40

[*The Grasshopper*]   69

To Lucasta. From Prison

AN EPODE

Long in thy shackles, liberty
I ask not from these walls, but thee,
Left for a while another's bride
To fancy all the world beside.

Yet ere I do begin to love,
See! how I all my objects prove;
Then my free soul to that confine
'Twere possible I might call mine.

First I would be in love with Peace,
And her rich swelling breasts increase;   10
But how, alas! how may that be,
Despising earth, she will love me?

Fain would I be in love with War,
As my dear just avenging star;
But War is loved so ev'rywhere,
Ev'n he disdains a lodging here.

Thee and thy wounds I would bemoan,
Fair thorough-shot Religiòn;
But he lives only that kills thee,
And whoso binds thy hands is free.   20

I would love a Parliament
As a main prop from Heav'n sent;
But ah! who's he that would be wedded
To th' fairest body that's beheaded?

Next would I court my Liberty,
And then my birthright, Property;
But can that be, when it is known
There's nothing you can call your own?

A Reformation I would have,

[*Richard Lovelace*]   70

As for our griefs a sov'reign salve;   30
That is, a cleansing of each wheel
Of state that yet some rust doth feel;

But not a Reformation so
As to reform were to o'erthrow;
Like watches by unskilful men
Disjointed, and set ill again.

The Public Faith I would adore,
But she is bankrupt of her store;
Nor how to trust her can I see,
For she that cozens all, must me.   40

Since then none of these can be
Fit objects for my love and me,
What then remains but th'only spring
Of all our loves and joys? The King.

He who, being the whole ball
Of day on earth, lends it to all;
When seeking to eclipse his right,
Blinded, we stand in our own light.

And now an universal mist
Of error is spread o'er each breast,   50
With such a fury edged, as is
Not found in th'inwards of th'Abyss.

Oh, from thy glorious starry wain
Dispense on me one sacred beam
To light me where I soon may see
How to serve you, and you trust me.

La Bella Bona Roba

I cannot tell who loves the skeleton
Of a poor marmoset, naught but bone, bone.
Give me a nakedness with her clothes on.

Such whose white-satin upper coat of skin,
Cut upon velvet rich incarnadin,
Has yet a body (and of flesh) within.

Sure it is meant good husbandry in men,
Who so incorporate with aery lean,
T' repair their sides, and get their rib again.

Hard hap unto that huntsman that decrees   10
Fat joys for all his sweat, whenas he sees,
After his 'say, naught but his keeper's fees.

Then Love, I beg, when next thou tak'st thy bow,
Thy angry shafts, and dost heart-chasing go,
Pass rascal deer, strike me the largest doe.

The Scrutiny

SONG

Why should you swear I am forsworn,
    Since thine I vowed to be?
Lady, it is already morn,
    And 'twas last night I swore to thee
That fond impossibility.

Have I not loved thee much and long,
    A tedious twelve hours' space?
I must all other beauties wrong,
    And rob thee of a new embrace,
Could I still dote upon thy face.   10

Not but all joy in thy brown hair,
    By others may be found;
But I must search the black and fair,
    Like skilful mineralists that sound
For treasure in unplowed-up ground.

Then, if when I have loved my round,

Thou prov'st the pleasant she,
With spoils of meaner beauties crowned,
   I laden will return to thee,
Ev'n sated with variety.   20

To Lucasta. The Rose

ODE

Sweet, serene sky-like flower,
Haste to adorn her bower;
   From thy long cloudy bed
   Shoot forth thy damask head.

New-startled blush of Flora!
The grief of pale Aurora,
   Who will contest no more,
   Haste, haste, to strow her floor.

Vermilion ball that's given
From lip to lip in heaven,   10
   Love's couch's coverled,
   Haste, haste, to make her bed.

Dear offspring of pleased Venus,
And jolly plump Silenus,
   Haste, haste, to deck the hair
   Of th' only sweetly fair.

See! rosy is her bower,
Her floor is all this flower;
   Her bed a rosy nest
   By a bed of roses pressed.   20

But early as she dresses,
Why fly you her bright tresses?
   Ah! I have found I fear,
   Because her cheeks are near.

To Lucasta. Going Beyond the Seas

SONG

If to be absent were to be
    Away from thee;
  Or that when I am gone,
  You or I were alone,
  Then, my Lucasta, might I crave
Pity from blustering wind or swallowing wave.

But I'll not sigh one blast or gale
    To swell my sail,
  Or pay a tear to 'suage
   The foaming blow-god's rage;   10
  For whether he will let me pass
Or no, I'm still as happy as I was.

Though seas and land betwixt us both,
    Our faith and troth,
  Like separated souls,
  All time and space controls;
  Above the highest sphere we meet,
Unseen, unknown, and greet as angels greet.

So then we do anticipate
    Our after-fate,   20
  And are alive i' the skies,
  If thus our lips and eyes
  Can speak like spirits unconfined
In Heav'n, their earthly bodies left behind.

To Lucasta. Going to the Wars

SONG

Tell me not (Sweet) I am unkind,
  That from the nunnery

[Richard Lovelace] 74

Of thy chaste breast and quiet mind
   To war and arms I fly.

True, a new mistress now I chase,
   The first foe in the field;
And with a stronger faith embrace
   A sword, a horse, a shield.

Yet this inconstancy is such
   As you too shall adore;   10
I could not love thee, dear, so much,
   Loved I not honor more.

Abraham Cowley

On the Death of Mr. Crashaw

Poet and saint! to thee alone are given
The two most sacred names of earth and heaven,
The hard and rarest union which can be,
Next that of Godhead with humanity.
Long did the Muses banished slaves abide,
And built vain pyramids to mortal pride;
Like Moses thou (though spells and charms withstand)
Hast brought them nobly home back to their Holy Land.
  Ah wretched we, poets of earth! but thou
Wert living the same poet which thou'rt now.   10
Whilst angels sing to thee their airs divine,
And joy in an applause so great as thine,
Equal society with them to hold,
Thou need'st not make new songs, but say the old.
And they, kind (spirits!) shall all rejoice to see
How little less than they, exalted man may be.
Still the old heathen gods in numbers dwell;
The heavenliest thing on earth still keeps up hell.
Nor have we yet quite purged the Christian land;
Still idols here, like calves at Bethel stand.   20
And though Pan's death long since all oracles broke,
Yet still in rhyme the fiend Apollo spoke:
Nay, with the worst of heathen dotage we
(Vain men!) the monster woman deify;
Find stars, and tie our fates there in a face,
And Paradise in them by whom we lost it, place.
What different faults corrupt our Muses thus?
Wanton as girls; as old wives, fabulous!
  Thy spotless Muse, like Mary, did contain
The boundless Godhead; she did well disdain   30
That her eternal verse employed should be
On a less subject than eternity;
And for a sacred mistress scorned to take

But her whom God himself scorned not His spouse to
    make.
It (in a kind) her miracle did do;
A fruitful mother was, and virgin too.
    How well (blest swan) did fate contrive thy death;
And made thee render up thy tuneful breath
In thy great mistress' arms; thou most divine
And richest offering of Loretto's shrine!   40
Where, like some holy sacrifice t' expire,
A fever burns thee, and love lights the fire.
Angels, they say, brought the famed chapel there,
And bore the sacred load in triumph through the air.
'Tis surer much they brought thee there; and they
And thou, their charge, went singing all the way.
    Pardon, my Mother Church, if I consent
That angels led him when from thee he went,
For even in error sure no danger is
When joined with so much piety as his.   50
Ah, mighty God, with shame I speak't, and grief,
Ah that our greatest faults were in belief!
And our weak reason were ev'n weaker yet,
Rather than thus our wills too strong for it.
His faith perhaps in some nice tenets might
Be wrong; his life, I'm sure, was in the right.
And I myself a Catholic will be,
So far at least, great saint, to pray to thee.
    Hail, bard triumphant, and some care bestow
On us, the poets militant below!   60
Opposed by our old enemy, adverse chance,
Attacked by envy, and by ignorance,
Enchained by beauty, tortured by desires,
Exposed by tyrant love to savage beasts and fires.
Thou from low earth in nobler flames didst rise,
And, like Elijah, mount alive the skies.
Elisha-like (but with a wish much less,
More fit thy greatness and my littleness),
Lo, here I beg (I whom thou once didst prove
So humble to esteem, so good to love)   70
Not that thy spirit might on me doubled be,

        [*On the Death of Mr. Crashaw*]   **77**

I ask but half thy mighty spirit for me
And when my Muse soars with so strong a wing,
'Twill learn of things divine, and first of thee to sing.

On the Death of Mr. William Hervey

Immodicis brevis est œtas, & rara senectus.

It was a dismal and a fearful night;
Scarce could the morn drive on the unwilling light,
When sleep, death's image, left my troubled breast,
   By something liker death possessed.
My eyes with tears did uncommanded flow,
    And on my soul hung the dull weight
    Of some intolerable fate.
What bell was that? Ah me! Too much I know.

My sweet companion, and my gentle peer,
Why hast thou left me thus unkindly here,   10
Thy end for ever, and my life to moan?
   Oh, thou hast left me all alone!
Thy soul and body, when death's agony
    Besieged around thy noble heart,
    Did not with more reluctance part
Then I, my dearest friend, do part from thee.

My dearest friend, would I had died for thee!
Life and this world henceforth will tedious be.
Nor shall I know hereafter what to do
    If once my griefs prove tedious too.   20
Silent and sad I walk about all day,
    As sullen ghosts stalk speechless by
    Where their hid treasures lie;
Alas, my treasure's gone; why do I stay?

He was my friend, the truest friend on earth;
A strong and mighty influence joined our birth.
Nor did we envy the most sounding name
    By friendship given of old to fame.
None but his brethren he, and sister, knew

Whom the kind youth preferred to me;   30
  And even in that we did agree,
For much above myself I loved them too.

Say, for you saw us, ye immortal lights,
How oft unwearied have we spent the nights?
Till the Ledæan stars, so famed for love,
  Wondered at us from above.
We spent them not in toys, in lusts, or wine,
  But search of deep philosophy,
  Wit, eloquence, and poetry,
Arts which I loved, for they, my friend, were thine.   40

Ye fields of Cambridge, our dear Cambridge, say,
Have ye not seen us walking every day?
Was there a tree about which did not know
  The love betwixt us two?
Henceforth, ye gentle trees, for ever fade;
  Or your sad branches thicker join,
  And into darksome shades combine,
Dark as the grave wherein my friend is laid.

Henceforth no learned youths beneath you sing,
Till all the tuneful birds to your boughs they bring;   50
No tuneful birds play with their wonted cheer,
  And call the learned youths to hear;
No whistling winds through the glad branches fly,
  But all with sad solemnity,
  Mute and unmovèd be,
Mute as the grave wherein my friend does lie.

To him my Muse made haste with every strain
Whilst it was new, and warm yet from the brain;
He loved my worthless rhymes, and like a friend
  Would find out something to commend.   60
Hence now, my Muse; thou canst not me delight;
  Be this my latest verse
  With which I now adorn his hearse,
And this my grief without thy help shall write.

Had I a wreath of bays about my brow,
I should contemn that flourishing honor now,
Condemn it to the fire, and joy to hear
    It rage and crackle there.
Instead of bays, crown with sad cypress me,
    Cypress which tombs does beautify;   70
    Not Phœbus grieved so much as I
For him who first was made that mournful tree.

Large was his soul; as large a soul as e'er
Submitted to inform a body here;
High as the place 'twas shortly in Heav'n to have,
    But low and humble as his grave;
So high that all the virtues there did come
    As to their chiefest seat,
    Conspicuous and great;
So low that for me, too, it made a room.   80

He scorned this busy world below, and all
That we, mistaken mortals, pleasure call;
Was filled with innocent gallantry and truth,
    Triumphant o'er the sins of youth.
He, like the stars, to which he now is gone,
    That shine with beams like flame,
    Yet burn not with the same,
Had all the light of youth, of the fire none.

Knowledge he only sought, and so soon caught,
As if for him knowledge had rather sought;   90
Nor did more learning ever crowded lie
    In such a short mortality.
Whene'er the skilful youth discoursed or writ,
    Still did the notions throng
    About his eloquent tongue,
Nor could his ink flow faster than his wit.

So strong a wit did nature to him frame
As all things but his judgment overcame;
His judgment like the heavenly moon did show,
    Tempering that mighty sea below.   100

        [Abraham Cowley] 80

Oh, had he lived in learning's world, what bound
    Would have been able to control
    His overpowering soul?
We have lost in him arts that not yet are found.

His mirth was the pure spirits of various wit,
Yet never did his God or friends forget.
And, when deep talk and wisdom came in view,
    Retired and gave to them their due.
For the rich help of books he always took,
    Though his own searching mind before   110
    Was so with notions written o'er
As if wise nature had made that her book.

So many virtues joined in him as we
Can scarce pick here and there in history,
More than old writers' practice e'er could reach,
    As much as they could ever teach.
These did religion, queen of virtues, sway,
    And all their sacred motions steer,
    Just like the first and highest sphere
Which wheels about, and turns all heav'n one way. 120

With as much zeal, devotion, piety,
He always lived, as other saints do die.
Still with his soul severe account he kept,
    Weeping all debts out ere he slept.
Then down in peace and innocence he lay,
    Like the sun's laborious light,
    Which still in water sets at night,
Unsullied with his journey of the day.

Wondrous young man, why wert thou made so good,
To be snatched hence ere better understood?   130
Snatched before half of thee enough was seen!
    Thou ripe, and yet thy life but green!
Nor could thy friends take their last sad farewell,
    But danger and infectious death
    Maliciously seized on that breath,
Where life, spirit, pleasure always used to dwell.

    [*On the Death of Mr. William Hervey*] 81

But happy thou, ta'en from this frantic age,
Where ignorance and hypocrisy does rage!
A fitter time for Heav'n no soul e'er chose,
    The place now only free from those.   140
There 'mong the blest thou dost for ever shine,
        And wheresoe'er thou casts thy view
        Upon that white and radiant crew,
Seest not a soul clothed with more light than thine.

And if the glorious saints cease not to know
Their wretched friends who fight with life below,
Thy flame to me does still the same abide,
    Only more pure and rarefied.
There whilst immortal hymns thou dost rehearse,
        Thou dost with holy pity see   150
        Our dull and earthly poesy,
Where grief and misery can be joined with verse.

Ode. Of Wit

Tell me, O tell, what kind of thing is wit,
    Thou who master art of it,
For the first matter loves variety less;
Less women love 't, either in love or dress.
    A thousand different shapes it bears,
    Comely in thousand shapes appears.
Yonder we saw it plain; and here 'tis now,
Like spirits in a place, we know not how.

London that vents of false ware so much store,
    In no ware deceives us more.   10
For men led by the color and the shape
Like Zeuxis' birds fly to the painted grape;
    Some things do through our judgment pass
    As through a multiplying glass.
And sometimes, if the object be too far,
We take a falling meteor for a star.

Hence 'tis a wit, that greatest word of fame,

Grows such a common name.
And wits by our creation they become
Just so as tit'lar bishops made at Rome.   20
  'Tis not a tale, 'tis not a jest
  Admired with laughter at a feast,
Nor florid talk, which can that title gain;
The proofs of wit forever must remain.

'Tis not to force some lifeless verses meet
  With their five gouty feet;
All ev'rywhere, like man's, must be the soul,
And reason the inferior powers control.
  Such were the numbers which could call
  The stones into the Theban wall.   30
Such miracles are ceased, and now we see
No towns or houses raised by poetry.

Yet 'tis not to adorn and gild each part;
  That shows more cost than art.
Jewels at nose and lips but ill appear;
Rather than all things wit, let none be there.
  Several lights will not be seen,
  If there be nothing else between.
Men doubt, because they stand so thick i' th' sky,
If those be stars which paint the galaxy.   40

'Tis not when two like words make up one noise;
  Jests for Dutchmen and English boys,
In which who finds out wit, the same may see
In an'grams and acrostics poetry.
  Much less can that have any place
  At which a virgin hides her face;
Such dross the fire must purge away; 'tis just
The author blush, there where the reader must.

'Tis not such lines as almost crack the stage
  When Bajazet begins to rage,   50
Nor a tall metaphor in the bombast way,
Nor the dry chips of short-lunged Seneca,

Nor upon all things to obtrude
And force some odd similitude.
What is it then which like the power divine
We only can by negatives define?

In a true piece of wit all things must be,
   Yet all things there agree;
As in the ark, joined without force or strife,
All creatures dwelt, all creatures that had life;   60
   Or as the primitive forms of all
   (If we compare great things with small)
Which without discord or confusion lie,
In that strange mirror of the deity.

But love that molds one man up out of two,
   Makes me forget and injure you.
I took you for myself sure when I thought
That you in anything were to be taught.
   Correct my error with thy pen;
   And if any ask me then,   70
What thing right wit and height of genius is,
I'll only show your lines and say, 'Tis this.

The Spring

Though you be absent here, I needs must say
The trees as beauteous are, and flowers as gay
   As ever they were wont to be;
   Nay, the birds' rural music too
   Is as melodious and free
   As if they sung to pleasure you;
I saw a rosebud ope this morn—I'll swear
The blushing morning opened not more fair.

How could it be so fair and you away?
How could the trees be beauteous, flowers so gay?   10
   Could they remember but last year
   How you did them, they you delight,
   The sprouting leaves which saw you here,

[Abraham Cowley] 84

And called their fellows to the sight,
Would, looking round for the same sight in vain,
Creep back into their silent barks again.

Where'er you walked, trees were as reverend made
As when of old gods dwelt in every shade.
   Is 't possible they should not know
   What loss of honor they sustain,   20
   That thus they smile and flourish now,
   And still their former pride retain?
Dull creatures! 'tis not without cause that she,
Who fled the god of wit, was made a tree.

In ancient times sure they much wiser were,
When they rejoiced the Thracian verse to hear;
   In vain did nature bid them stay,
   When Orpheus had his song begun;
   They called their wond'ring roots away,
   And bade them silent to him run.   30
How would those learned trees have followed you?
You would have drawn them, and their poet too.

But who can blame them now? for, since you're gone,
They're here the only fair, and shine alone.
   You did their natural rights invade:
   Wherever you did walk or sit,
   The thickest boughs could make no shade,
   Although the sun had granted it;
The fairest flowers could please no more, near you,
Than painted flowers, set next to them, could do.   40

Whene'er then you come hither, that shall be
The time, which this to others is, to me.
   The little joys which here are now,
   The name of punishments do bear;
   When by their sight they let us know
   How we deprived of greater are.
'Tis you the best of seasons with you bring;
This is for beasts, and that for men the spring.

Beauty

Beauty, thou wild fantastic ape,
　　Who dost in ev'ry country change thy shape!
Here black, there brown, here tawny, and there white;
Thou flatt'rer which compli'st with every sight!
　　Thou Babel which confound'st the eye
With unintelligible variety!
　　Who hast no certain what, nor where,
But variest still, and dost thy self declare
Inconstant, as thy she-professors are.

　　Beauty, Love's scene and masquerade,　　　　　10
So gay by well-plac'd lights, and distance made;
False coin, with which th' imposter cheats us still;
The stamp and color good, but metal ill!
　　Which light, or base we find, when we
Weigh by enjoyment, and examine thee!
　　For though thy being be but show,
'Tis chiefly night which men to thee allow:
And choose t'enjoy thee, when thou least art thou.
　　Beauty, thou active, passive ill!
Which diest thy self as fast as thou dost kill!　　20
Thou tulip, who thy stock in paint dost waste,
Neither for physic good, nor smell, nor taste.
　　Beauty, whose flames but meteors are,
Short-liv'd and low, though thou wouldst seem a star,
　　Who dar'st not thine own home descry,
Pretending to dwell richly in the eye,
When thou, alas, dost in the Fancy lye.

　　Beauty, whose conquests still are made
O'er hearts by cowards kept, or else betray'd!
Weak victor! who thy self destroy'd must be　　30
When sickness, storms, or time besieges thee!
　　Thou, unwholesome thaw to frozen age!
Thou strong wine, which youth's feaver dost enrage,
　　Thou tyrant which leav'st no man free!

[*Abraham Cowley*] 86

Thou subtle thief, from whom nought safe can be!
Thou murd'rer which hast kill'd, and devil which wouldst
     damn me.

My Picture

Here, take my likeness with you, whilst 'tis so;
          For when from hence you go,
               The next sun's rising will behold
               Me pale, and lean, and old.
          The man who did this picture draw,
Will swear next day my face he never saw.

I really believe, within a while,
          If you upon this shadow smile,
               Your presence will such vigor give,
               (Your presence which makes all things live)   10
          And absence so much alter me,
This will be the substance, I the shadow be.

When from your well-wrought cabinet you take it,
          And your bright looks awake it;
               Ah be not frighted, if you see,
               The new-soul'd picture gaze on thee,
          And here it breathe a sigh or two;
For those are the first things that it will do.

My rival-image will be then thought blest,
          And laugh at me as dispossessed;   20
               But, thou, who (if I know thee right)
               I'th' substance dost not much delight,
          Wilt rather send again for me,
Who then shall but my picture's picture be.

Richard Crashaw

Upon Two Green Apricots Sent
to Cowley by Sir Crashaw

Take these, time's tardy truants, sent by me,
To be chastis'd (sweet friend) and chid by thee.
Pale sons of our Pomona! whose wan cheeks
Have spent the patience of expecting weeks,
Yet are scarce ripe enough at best to show
The red, but of the blush to thee they owe.
By thy comparison they shall put on
More summer in their shame's reflection
Than e'er the fruitful Phoebus' flaming kisses
Kindled on their cold lips. O had my wishes   10
And the dear merits of your Muse their due,
The year had found some fruit early as you:
Ripe as those rich composures time computes
Blossoms, but our blessed taste confesses fruits.
How does thy April-autumn mock these cold
Progressions 'twixt whose terms poor time grows old?
With thee alone he wears no beard, thy brain
Gives him the morning world's fresh gold again.
'Twas only Paradise, 'tis only thou,
Whose fruit and blossoms both bless the same bough. 20
Proud in the pattern of thy precious youth,
Nature (methinks) might easily mend her growth.
Could she in all her births but copy thee,
Into the public year's proficiency,
No fruit should have the face to smile on thee
(Young master of the world's maturity)
But such whose sun-born beauties what they borrow
Of beams today, pay back again tomorrow,
Nor need be double-gilt. How then must these
Poor fruits look pale at thy Hesperides!   30
Fain would I chide their slowness, but in their
Defects I draw mine own dull character.
Take them, and me in them acknowledging,
How much my summer waits upon thy spring.

Wishes to His (Supposed) Mistress

Whoe'er she be,
That not impossible she,
That shall command my heart and me;

Where'er she lie,
Locked up from mortal eye,
In shady leaves of destiny,

Till that ripe birth
Of studied fate stand forth,
And teach her fair steps to our earth;

Till that divine   10
Idea take a shrine
Of crystal flesh, through which to shine;

Meet you her, my wishes,
Bespeak her to my blisses,
And be ye called my absent kisses.

I wish her beauty,
That owes not all his duty
To gaudy tire, or glist'ring shoe-tie;

Something more than
Taffeta or tissue can,   20
Or rampant feather, or rich fan;

More than the spoil
Of shop, or silkworm's toil,
Or a bought blush, or a set smile;

A face that's best
By its own beauty dressed,
And can alone command the rest;

[*Wishes to His (Supposed) Mistress*] 89

A face made up
Out of no other shop
Than what nature's white hand sets ope;   30

A cheek where youth
And blood, with pen of truth
Write, what the reader sweetly ru'th;

A cheek where grows
More than a morning rose,
Which to no box his being owes;

Lips where all day
A lover's kiss may play,
Yet carry nothing thence away;

Looks that oppress   40
Their richest tires, but dress
And clothe their simplest nakedness.

Eyes that displace
The neighbor diamond, and out-face
That sunshine by their own sweet grace;

Tresses that wear
Jewels but to declare
How much themselves more precious are;

Whose native ray
Can tame the wanton day   50
Of gems, that in their bright shades play—

Each ruby there,
Or pearl that dare appear,
Be its own blush, be its own tear;

A well-tamed heart,
For whose more noble smart,
Love may be long choosing a dart;

[*Richard Crashaw*]   90

Eyes that bestow
Full quivers on love's bow,
Yet pay less arrows than they owe;   60

Smiles that can warm
The blood, yet teach a charm,
That chastity shall take no harm;

Blushes that bin
The burnish of no sin,
Nor flames of aught too hot within;

Joys that confess
Virtue their mistress,
And have no other head to dress;

Fears, fond and flight,   70
As the coy bride's, when night
First does the longing lover right;

Tears, quickly fled
And vain, as those are shed
For a dying maidenhead;

Days that need borrow
No part of their good morrow
From a fore-spent night of sorrow;

Days that, in spite
Of darkness, by the light   80
Of a clear mind are day all night;

Nights sweet as they,
Made short by lovers' play,
Yet long by th' absence of the day;

Life that dares send
A challenge to his end,
And when it comes say, "Welcome, friend!"

[*Wishes to His (Supposed) Mistress*]   **91**

Sidneian showers
Of sweet discourse, whose powers
Can crown old winter's head with flowers;   90

Soft silken hours,
Open suns, shady bowers;
'Bove all, nothing within that lowers;

Whate'er delight
Can make day's forehead bright,
Or give down to the wings of night.

In her whole frame
Have nature all the name,
Art and ornament the shame.

Her flattery,   100
Picture and poesy:
Her counsel her own virtue be.

I wish her store
Of worth may leave her poor
Of wishes; and I wish—no more.

Now if time knows
That her whose radiant brows
Weave them a garland of my vows;

Her whose just bays
My future hopes can raise,   110
A trophy to her present praise;

Her that dares be
What these lines wish to see:
I seek no further, it is she.

'Tis she, and here
Lo! I unclothe and clear
My wishes' cloudy character.

May she enjoy it
Whose merit dare apply it,
But modesty dares still deny it.   120

Such worth as this is
Shall fix my flying wishes,
And determine them to kisses.

Let her full glory,
My fancies, fly before ye!
Be ye my fictions, but her story.

In the Holy Nativity of Our Lord God

A Hymn Sung as by the Shepherds

CHORUS

Come, we shepherds whose blest sight
Hath met love's noon in nature's night;
Come, lift we up our loftier song
And wake the sun that lies too long.

To all our world of well-stol'n joy
    He slept, and dreamed of no such thing,
While we found out Heaven's fairer eye,
    And kissed the cradle of our King.
Tell him he rises now too late
To show us aught worth looking at.   10

Tell him we now can show him more
    Than he e'er showed to mortal sight,
Than he himself e'er saw before,
    Which to be seen needs not his light.
Tell him, Tityrus, where th' hast been;
Tell him, Thyrsis, what th' hast seen.

Tityrus

Gloomy night embraced the place
    Where the noble infant lay;

The babe looked up and showed his face:
  In spite of darkness, it was day.   20
It was thy day, Sweet, and did rise
Not from the east, but from thine eyes.

  Chorus. It was thy day, Sweet, [etc.]

  Thyrsis

Winter chid aloud, and sent
  The angry north to wage his wars.
The north forgot his fierce intent,
  And left perfumes instead of scars.
By those sweet eyes' persuasive pow'rs,
Where he meant frost, he scattered flowers.

  Chorus. By those sweet eyes' [etc.]   30

  Both

We saw thee in thy balmy nest,
  Young dawn of our eternal day!
We saw thine eyes break from their east
  And chase the trembling shades away.
We saw thee, and we blessed the sight;
We saw thee by thine own sweet light.

  Tityrus

"Poor world," said I, "what wilt thou do
  To entertain this starry Stranger?
Is this the best thou canst bestow,
  A cold and not too cleanly manger?   40
Contend, ye powers of heav'n and earth,
To fit a bed for this huge birth!"

  Chorus. Contend, ye powers [etc.]

  Thyrsis

"Proud world," said I, "cease your contest,
  And let the mighty babe alone.
The phoenix builds the phoenix' nest.
  Love's architecture is His own.
                              [*Richard Crashaw*] 94

The babe whose birth embraves this morn
Made his own bed ere he was born."

    Chorus. The Babe whose birth [etc.]   50

    Tityrus

I saw the curled drops, soft and slow,
   Come hovering o'er the place's head,
Off'ring their whitest sheets of snow
   To furnish the fair infant's bed.
"Forbear," said I, "be not too bold;
Your fleece is white, but 'tis too cold."

    Chorus. "Forbear," said I, [etc.]

    Thyrsis

I saw the obsequious seraphims
   Their rosy fleece of fire bestow;
For well they now can spare their wings,   60
   Since Heav'n itself lies here below.
"Well done," said I, "but are you sure
Your down so warm will pass for pure?"

    Chorus. "Well done," said I, [etc.]

    Tityrus

No, no, your king's not yet to seek
   Where to repose his royal head;
See, see, how soon his new-bloomed cheek
   'Twixt mother's breasts is gone to bed.
"Sweet choice!" said we, "no way but so,
Not to lie cold, yet sleep in snow."   70

    Chorus. "Sweet choice!" said we, [etc.]

    Both

We saw thee in thy balmy nest,
   Bright dawn of our eternal day!
We saw thine eyes break from their east

    [*In the Holy Nativity of Our Lord God*]   95

And chase the trembling shades away.
We saw thee, and we blessed the sight;
We saw thee by thine own sweet light.

Chorus. We saw thee, [etc.]

Full Chorus

Welcome, all wonders in one sight!
 Eternity shut in a span,   80
Summer in winter, day in night,
 Heaven in earth, and God in man.
Great little one, whose all-embracing birth
Lifts earth to Heaven, stoops Heav'n to earth.

Welcome, though nor to gold nor silk,
 To more than Caesar's birthright is;
Two sister-seas of virgin-milk,
 With many a rarely tempered kiss,
That breathes at once both maid and mother,
Warms in the one, cools in the other.   90

Welcome, though not to those gay flies
 Gilded i'th'beams of earthly kings,
Slippery souls in smiling eyes;
 But to poor shepherds, homespun things,
Whose wealth's their flock, whose wit, to be
 Well read in their simplicity.
Yet when young April's husband-showers
 Shall bless the fruitful Maia's bed,
We'll bring the first-born of her flowers
 To kiss thy feet and crown thy head.   100
To thee, dread lamb! whose love must keep
 The shepherds more than they the sheep;
To thee, meek majesty! soft king
 Of simple graces and sweet loves,
Each of us his lamb will bring,
 Each his pair of silver doves;
Till burnt at last in fire of thy fair eyes,
 Ourselves become our own best sacrifice.

On Mr. G. Herbert's Book, Entitled The Temple of Sacred Poems, Sent to a Gentlewoman

Know you, fair, on what you look:
Divinest love lies in this book,
Expecting fire from your eyes
To kindle this his sacrifice.
When your hands untie these strings,
Think you have an angel by th' wings
One that gladly will be nigh
To wait upon each morning sigh,
To flutter in the balmy air
Of your well-perfumed prayer.   10
These white plumes of his he'll lend you,
Which every day to heaven will send you
To take acquaintance of the sphere,
And all the smooth-faced kindred there,
And though Herbert's name do owe
These devotions, fairest, know
That while I lay them on the shrine
Of your white hand, they are mine.

To the Noblest and Best of Ladies, the Countess of Denbigh

> *Persuading her to resolution in religion, and to render herself without further delay into the communion of the Catholic Church*

What Heaven-entreated heart is this?
Stands trembling at the gate of bliss;
Holds fast the door, yet dares not venture
Fairly to open it, and enter;
Whose definition is a doubt
'Twixt life and death, 'twixt in and out.
Say, lingering fair! why comes the birth
Of your brave soul so slowly forth?
Plead your pretenses, o you strong

In weakness! why you choose so long　　　　　10
In labor of yourself to lie,
Not daring quite to live nor die?
Ah, linger not, loved soul! A slow
And late consent was a long no;
Who grants at last, long time tried
And did his best to have denied.
What magic bolts, what mystic bars
Maintain the will in these strange wars!
What fatal, yet fantastic, bands
Keep the free heart from its own hands!　　　20
So when the year takes cold we see
Poor waters their own prisoners be.
Fettered and locked up fast they lie
In a sad self-captivity.
The astonished nymphs their flood's strange fate deplore,
To see themselves their own severer shore.
Thou that alone canst thaw this cold,
And fetch the heart from its stronghold,
Almighty Love! end this long war,
And of a meteor make a star.　　　　　　　30
Oh, fix this fair indefinite,
And 'mongst thy shafts of sovereign light
Choose out that sure decisive dart
Which has the key of this close heart,
Knows all the corners of 't, and can control
The self-shut cabinet of an unsearched soul.
Oh, let it be at last Love's hour;
Raise this tall trophy of thy pow'r;
Come once the conquering way, not to confute
But kill this rebel-word, "irresolute,"　　　40
That so, in spite of all this peevish strength
Of weakness, she may write, "Resolved at length."
Unfold at length, unfold, fair flower,
And use the season of Love's shower;
Meet his well-meaning wounds, wise heart!
And haste to drink the wholesome dart,
That healing shaft, which Heav'n till now
Hath in love's quiver hid for you.
O dart of Love! arrow of light!

O happy you, if it hit right!   50
It must not fall in vain, it must
Not mark the dry regardless dust.
Fair one, it is your fate, and brings
Eternal worlds upon its wings.
Meet it with wide-spread arms, and see
Its seat your soul's just center be.
Disband dull fears, give faith the day;
To save your life, kill your delay.
It is Love's siege, and sure to be
Your triumph, through his victory.   60
'Tis cowardice that keeps this field,
And want of courage not to yield.
Yield then, O yield, that Love may win
The fort at last, and let life in.
Yield quickly. Lest perhaps you prove
Death's prey, before the prize of Love.
This fort of your fair self, if 't be not won,
He is repulsed indeed, but you're undone.

A Hymn to the Name and Honor of the Admirable Saint Teresa

> *Foundress of the Reformation of the Discalced*
> *Carmelites, both men and women. A woman*
> *for angelical height of speculation, for*
> *masculine courage of performance,*
> *more than a woman; who yet a*
> *child outran maturity, and durst*
> *plot a martyrdom.*

Love, thou art absolute sole lord
Of life and death. To prove the word,
We'll now appeal to none of all
Those thy old soldiers, great and tall,
Ripe men of martyrdom, that could reach down
With strong arms their triumphant crown;
Such as could with lusty breath
Speak loud into the face of death
Their great Lord's glorious name; to none

Of those whose spacious bosoms spread a throne 10
For Love at large to fill. Spare blood and sweat,
And see Him take a private seat,
Making His mansion in the mild
And milky soul of a soft child.

Scarce has she learnt to lisp the name
Of martyr, yet she thinks it shame
Life should so long play with that breath
Which spent can buy so brave a death.
She never undertook to know
What death with Love should have to do; 20
Nor has she e'er yet understood
Why to show love she should shed blood;
Yet though she cannot tell you why,
She can love and she can die.

Scarce has she blood enough to make
A guilty sword blush for her sake;
Yet has she a heart dares hope to prove
How much less strong is death than Love.

Be Love but there: let poor six years
Be posed with the maturest fears 30
Man trembles at, you straight shall find
Love knows no nonage, nor the mind.
'Tis Love, not years or limbs, that can
Make the martyr or the man.

Love touched her heart, and lo it beats
High, and burns with such brave heats,
Such thirsts to die, as dares drink up
A thousand cold deaths in one cup.
Good reason. For she breathes all fire.
Her weak breast heaves with strong desire 40
Of what she may with fruitless wishes
Seek for amongst her mother's kisses.

Since 'tis not to be had at home,
She'll travel to a martyrdom.
No home for hers confesses she
But where she may a martyr be.

She'll to the Moors, and trade with them
For this unvalued diadem.
She'll offer them her dearest breath,

With Christ's name in 't, in change for death.　　50
She'll bargain with them, and will give
Them God, teach them how to live
In him; or, if they this deny,
For him she'll teach them how to die.
So shall she leave amongst them sown
Her Lord's blood, or at least her own.
　　Farewell then, all the world, adieu!
Teresa is no more for you.
Farewell, all pleasures, sports, and joys,
(Never till now esteemèd toys)　　　　60
Farewell, whatever dear may be,
Mother's arms, or father's knee;
Farewell house, and farewell home!
She's for the Moors and martyrdom.
　　Sweet, not so fast! lo, thy fair Spouse
Whom thou seek'st with so swift vows
Calls thee back, and bids thee come
T' embrace a milder martyrdom.
　　Blest powers forbid thy tender life
Should bleed upon a barbarous knife;　　70
Or some base hand have power to rase
Thy breast's chaste cabinet, and uncase
A soul kept there so sweet; oh no,
Wise Heav'n will never have it so:
Thou art Love's victim, and must die
A death more mystical and high;
Into Love's arms thou shalt let fall
A still surviving funeral.
His is the dart must make the death
Whose stroke shall taste thy hallowed breath;　　80
A dart thrice dipped in that rich flame
Which writes thy spouse's radiant name
Upon the roof of Heav'n, where aye
It shines, and with a sovereign ray
Beats bright upon the burning faces
Of souls which in that name's sweet graces
Find everlasting smiles. So rare,
So spiritual, pure, and fair
Must be th' immortal instrument

Upon whose choice point shall be sent 90
A life so loved; and that there be
Fit executioners for thee,
The fair'st and first-born sons of fire,
Blest seraphim, shall leave their choir
And turn Love's soldiers, upon thee
To exercise their archery.
   Oh, how oft shalt thou complain
Of a sweet and subtle pain,
Of intolerable joys,
Of a death in which who dies 100
Loves his death, and dies again,
And would for ever so be slain,
And lives and dies, and knows not why
To live, but that he thus may never leave to die!
   How kindly will thy gentle heart
Kiss the sweetly killing dart!
And close in his embraces keep
Those delicious wounds, that weep
Balsam to heal themselves with. Thus
When these thy deaths, so numerous, 110
Shall all at last die into one,
And melt thy soul's sweet mansion;
Like a soft lump of incense, hasted
By too hot a fire, and wasted
Into perfuming clouds, so fast
Shalt thou exhale to Heav'n at last
In a resolving sigh, and then,
Oh, what? Ask not the tongues of men
Angels cannot tell; suffice,
Thyself shall feel thine own full joys 120
And hold them fast for ever. There
So soon as thou shalt first appear,
The moon of maiden stars, thy white
Mistress, attended by such bright
Souls as thy shining self, shall come
And in her first ranks make thee room;
Where 'mongst her snowy family
Immortal welcomes wait for thee.
   Oh, what delight when revealed life shall stand

And teach thy lips Heav'n with his hand,   130
On which thou now mayst to thy wishes
Heap up thy consecrated kisses.
What joys shall seize thy soul when she,
Bending her blessed eyes on thee,
(Those second smiles of Heav'n) shall dart
Her mild rays through thy melting heart!
    Angels, thy old friends, there shall greet thee,
Glad at their own home now to meet thee.
    All thy good works which went before
And waited for thee, at the door,   140
Shall own thee there, and all in one
Weave a constellation
Of crowns, with which the king, thy spouse,
Shall build up thy triumphant brows.
    All thy old woes shall now smile on thee,
And thy pains sit bright upon thee;
All thy sorrows here shall shine,
All thy sufferings be divine.
Tears shall take comfort and turn gems,
And wrongs repent to diadems.   150
Even thy deaths shall live, and new
Dress the soul that erst they slew
Thy wounds shall blush to such bright scars
As keep account of the lamb's wars.
    Those rare works where thou shalt leave writ
Love's noble history, with wit
Taught thee by none but Him, while here
They feed our souls, shall clothe thine there.
Each heav'nly word by whose hid flame
Our hard hearts shall strike fire, the same   160
Shall flourish on thy brows, and be
Both fire to us and flame to thee,
Whose light shall live bright in thy face
By glory, in our hearts by grace.
    Thou shalt look round about and see
Thousands of crowned souls throng to be
Themselves thy crown. Sons of thy vows,
The virgin-births with which thy sovereign Spouse
Made fruitful thy fair soul, go now

[A Hymn to ... the Admirable Saint Teresa]   103

And with them all about thee bow 170
To Him. "Put on," He'll say, "put on
(My rosy love) that thy rich zone
Sparkling with the sacred flames
Of thousand souls, whose happy names
Heav'n keeps upon thy score. (Thy bright
Life brought them first to kiss the light
That kindled them to stars)." And so
Thou with the lamb, thy lord, shalt go,
And whereso'er he sets his white
Steps, walk with him those ways of light 180
Which who in death would live to see
Must learn in life to die like thee.

A Song

Lord, when the sense of thy sweet grace
Sends up my soul to seek thy face,
Thy blessed eyes breed such desire,
I die in Love's delicious fire.
   O Love, I am thy sacrifice.
Be still triumphant, blessed eyes.
Still shine on me, fair suns! that I
Still may behold, though still I die.

SECOND PART

Though still I die, I live again;
Still longing so to be still slain, 10
So gainful is such loss of breath,
I die even in desire of death.
   Still live in me this loving strife   .
Of living death and dying life.
For while thou sweetly slayest me,
Dead to myself, I live in thee.

Upon the Infant Martyrs

To see both blended in one flood,
The mothers' milk, the children's blood,

Makes me doubt if Heaven will gather
Roses hence, or lilies rather.

John III

BUT MEN LOVED DARKNESS RATHER THAN LIGHT

The world's light shines, shine as it will,
The world will love its darkness still;
I doubt though when the world's in hell,
It will not love its darkness half so well.

Mark XII

GIVE TO CAESAR ... AND TO GOD ...

All we have is God's, and yet
Caesar challenges a debt,
Nor hath God a thinner share,
Whatever Caesar's payments are;
All is God's; and yet, 'tis true
All we have is Caesar's too;
All is Caesar's; and what odds
So long as Caesar's self is God's?

Upon Bishop Andrews,
His Picture Before His Sermons

This reverend shadow cast that setting sun,
Whose glorious course through our horizon run,
Left the dim face of this dull hemisphere
All one great eye, all drown'd in one great tear.
Whose fair illustrious soul led his free thought
Through learning's universe, and (vainly) sought
Room for her spacious self, until at length
She found the way home, with an holy strength
Snatch'd her self hence, to Heaven; fill'd a bright place
'Mongst those immortal fires, and on the face   10
Of her great maker fix'd her flaming eye,

There still to read true pure divinity.
And now that grave aspect hath deign'd to shrink
Into this less appearance. If you think
'Tis but a dead face, art doth here bequeath:
Look on the following leaves, and see him breathe.

Henry Vaughan

Regeneration

A ward, and still in bonds, one day
    I stole abroad;
It was high spring, and all the way
  Primrosed and hung with shade;
   Yet was it frost within,
     And surly winds
Blasted my infant buds, and sin
  Like clouds eclipsed my mind.

Stormed thus, I straight perceived my spring
    Mere stage and show,   10
My walk a monstrous, mountained thing,
  Rough-cast with rocks and snow;
   And as a pilgrim's eye
     Far from relief,
Measures the melancholy sky,
  Then drops and rains for grief,

So sighed I upwards still; at last
    'Twixt steps and falls
I reached the pinnacle, where placed
  I found a pair of scales;   20
   I took them up and laid
     In th' one late pains;
The other smoke and pleasures weighed,
  But proved the heavier grains;

With that, some cried, "Away!" Straight I
    Obeyed, and led
Full east, a fair, fresh field could spy;
  Some called it Jacob's bed,
  A virgin soil which no
     Rude feet ere trod,   30
Where (since he stepped there) only go
  Prophets, and friends of God.

Here, I reposed; but scarce well set,
  A grove descried
Of stately height, whose branches met
  And mixed on every side;
  I entered, and once in,
  (Amazed to see 't,)
Found all was changed, and a new spring
  Did all my senses greet;   40

The unthrift sun shot vital gold,
  A thousand pieces,
And heaven its azure did unfold,
  Checkered with snowy fleeces;
  The air was all in spice,
  And every bush
A garland wore; thus fed my eyes,
  But all the ear lay hush.

Only a little fountain lent
  Some use for ears,   50
And on the dumb shades language spent,
  The music of her tears;
  I drew her near, and found
  The cistern full
Of divers stones, some bright and round,
  Others ill-shaped and dull.

The first (pray mark) as quick as light
  Danced through the flood,
But, the last, more heavy than the night,
  Nailed to the center stood;   60
  I wondered much, but tired
  At last with thought,
My restless eye that still desired
  As strange an object brought;

It was a bank of flowers, where I descried,
  (Though 'twas midday,)
Some fast asleep, others broad-eyed
  And taking in the ray;

Here musing long, I heard
    A rushing wind   70
Which still increased, but whence it stirred
  No where I could not find;

I turned me round, and to each shade
    Dispatched an eye
To see if any leaf had made
  Least motion, or reply,
  But while I list'ning sought
    My mind to ease
By knowing where 'twas, or where not,
  It whispered, "Where I please."   80

"Lord," then said I, "on me one breath,
And let me die before my death!"

The Dawning

Ah! what time wilt Thou come? when shall that cry,
"The bridegroom's coming," fill the sky?
Shall it in the evening run,
When our words and works are done?
Or will thy all-surprising light
    Break at midnight?
When either sleep or some dark pleasure
Possesseth mad man without measure;
Or shall these early fragrant hours
    Unlock thy bowers?   10
And with their blush of light descry
Thy locks crowned with eternity.
Indeed, it is the only time
That with thy glory doth best chime;
All now are stirring, ev'ry field
    Full hymns doth yield,
The whole creation shakes off night,
And for thy shadow looks the light;
Stars now vanish without number,
Sleepy planets set and slumber,   20

The pursy clouds disband and scatter,
All expect some sudden matter;
Not one beam triumphs, but from far
      That morning star.
Oh, at what time soever, Thou,
(Unknown to us) the heavens wilt bow,
And, with thy angels in the van,
Descend to judge poor careless man,
Grant, I may not like puddle lie
In a corrupt security,   30
Where, if a traveler water crave,
He finds it dead and in a grave;
But as this restless vocal spring
All day and night doth run and sing,
And though here born, yet is acquainted
Elsewhere, and flowing keeps untainted;
So let me all my busy age
In thy free services engage;
And though while here of force I must
Have commerce sometimes with poor dust, 40
And in my flesh, though vile and low,
As this doth in her channel, flow,
Yet let my course, my aim, my love,
And chief acquaintance be above;
So when that day and hour shall come
In which thyself will be the sun,
Thou'lt find me dressed and on my way,
Watching the break of thy great Day.

The Retreat

Happy those early days, when I
Shined in my angel infancy;
Before I understood this place
Appointed for my second race,
Or taught my soul to fancy aught
But a white, celestial thought;
When yet I had not walked above

[Henry Vaughan] 110

A mile, or two, from my first love,
And looking back, (at that short space,)
Could see a glimpse of his bright face;   10
When on some gilded cloud or flower
My gazing soul would dwell an hour,
And in those weaker glories spy
Some shadows of eternity;
Before I taught my tongue to wound
My conscience with a sinful sound,
Or had the black art to dispense
A sev'ral sin to every sense,
But felt through all this fleshly dress
Bright shoots of everlastingness.   20
    Oh, how I long to travel back,
And tread again that ancient track!
That I might once more reach that plain
Where first I left my glorious train;
From whence the enlightened spirit sees
That shady city of palm trees.
But (ah!) my soul with too much stay
Is drunk, and staggers in the way.
Some men a forward motion love,
But I by backward steps would move,   30
And when this dust falls to the urn
In that state I came, return.

Peace

My soul, there is a country
    Far beyond the stars,
Where stands a wingèd sentry
    All skilful in the wars.
There above noise and danger,
    Sweet peace sits crowned with smiles,
And one born in a manger
    Commands the beauteous files.
He is thy gracious friend,
    And (O my soul, awake!)   10
Did in pure love descend

To die here for thy sake.
If thou canst get but thither,
    There grows the flower of peace,
The rose that cannot wither,
    Thy fortress and thy ease.
Leave then thy foolish ranges;
    For none can thee secure,
But one, who never changes,
    Thy God, thy life, thy cure.   20

Love-sick

Jesus, my life! how shall I truly love thee?
O that thy Spirit would so strongly move me,
That thou wert pleased to shed thy grace so far
As to make man all pure love, flesh a star!
A star that would ne'er set, but ever rise,
So rise and run, as to out-run these skies,
These narrow skies (narrow to me) that bar,
So bar me in, that I am still at war,
At constant war with them. O come and rend,
Or bow the heavens! Lord, bow them and descend,   10
And at thy presence make these mountains flow,
These mountains of cold ice in me! Thou art
Refining fire, O then refine my heart,
My foul, foul heart! Thou art immortal heat,
Heat motion gives; then warm it till it beat,
So beat for thee, till thou in mercy hear,
So hear that thou must open: open to
A sinful wretch, a wretch that caused thy woe,
Thy woe, who caused his weal; so far his weal
That thou forgot'st thine own, for thou didst seal   20
Mine with thy blood, thy blood which makes thee mine,
Mine ever, ever; and me ever thine.

The Morning Watch

O joys! infinite sweetness! with what flowers,
And shoots of glory, my soul breaks, and buds!

[Henry Vaughan]   112

<pre>
                    All the long hours
                    Of night, and rest
                    Through the still shrouds
                    Of sleep, and clouds,
        This dew fell on my breast;
                    O how it bloods,
And spirits all my earth! heark! in what rings,
And hymning circulations the quick world   10
                    Awakes, and sings;
                    The rising winds,
                    And falling springs,
                    Birds, beasts, all things
        Adore him in their kinds.
                    Thus all is hurled
In sacred hymns, and order, the great chime
And symphony of nature. Prayer is
                    The world in tune,
                    A spirit-voice,   20
                    And vocal joys
        Whose echo is Heav'n's bliss.
                    O let me climb
When I lie down! The pious soul by night
Is like a clouded star, whose beams though said
                    To shed their light
                    Under some cloud
                    Yet are above,
                    And shine, and move   30
        Beyond that misty shroud.
                    So in my bed
That curtained grave, though sleep, like ashes, hide
My lamp, and life, both shall in thee abide.
</pre>

The Waterfall

<pre>
With what deep murmurs through time's silent stealth
Doth thy transparent, cool and wat'ry wealth
                    Here flowing fall,
                    And chide, and call,
</pre>

As if his liquid, loose retinue staid
Ling'ring, and were of this steep place afraid,
  The common pass
  Where, clear as glass,
  All must descend
  Not to an end: 10
But quick'ned by this deep and rocky grave,
Rise to a longer course more bright and brave.

  Dear stream! dear bank, where often I
  Have sat, and pleased my pensive eye,
  Why, since each drop of thy quick store
  Runs thither, whence it flowed before,
  Should poor souls fear a shade or night,
  Who came (sure) from a sea of light?
  Or since those drops are all sent back
  So sure to thee, that none doth lack, 20
  Why should frail flesh doubt any more
  That what God takes, he'll not restore?

  O useful element and clear!
  My sacred wash and cleanser here,
  My first consigner unto those
  Fountains of life, where the lamb goes!
  What sublime truths and wholesome themes
  Lodge in thy mystical, deep streams!
  Such as dull man can never find
  Unless that Spirit lead his mind   30
  Which first upon thy face did move,
  And hatched all with his quickening love.
  As this loud brook's incessant fall
  In streaming rings restagnates all,
  Which reach by course the bank, and then
  Are no more seen, just so pass men.
  O my invisible estate,
  My glorious liberty, still late!
  Thou art the channel my soul seeks,
  Not this with cataracts and creeks. 40

The Night

    Through that pure virgin shrine,
That sacred veil drawn o'er thy glorious noon,
That men might look and live, as glowworms shine,
        And face the moon,
    Wise Nicodemus saw such light
    As made him know his God by night.

    Most blest believer he!
Who in that land of darkness and blind eyes
Thy long-expected healing wings could see,
        When Thou didst rise,   10
    And, what can never more be done,
    Did at midnight speak with the sun!

    Oh who will tell me where
He found Thee at that dead and silent hour!
What hallowed solitary ground did bear
        So rare a flower,
    Within whose sacred leaves did lie
    The fulness of the Deity?

    No mercy-seat of gold,
No dead and dusty cherub, nor carved stone,   20
But His own living works did my Lord hold
        And lodge alone;
    Where trees and herbs did watch and peep
    And wonder, while the Jews did sleep.

    Dear night! this world's defeat;
The stop to busy fools; care's check and curb;
The day of spirits; my soul's calm retreat
        Which none disturb!
    Christ's progress, and His prayer time;
    The hours to which high Heaven doth chime;   30

    God's silent, searching flight;

When my Lord's head is filled with dew, and all
His locks are wet with the clear drops of night;
  His still, soft call;
  His knocking time; the soul's dumb watch,
  When spirits their fair kindred catch.

  Were all my loud, evil days
Calm and unhaunted as is thy dark tent,
Whose peace but by some angel's wing or voice
  Is seldom rent,   40
  Then I in heaven all the long year
  Would keep, and never wander here.

  But living where the sun
Doth all things wake, and where all mix and tire
Themselves and others, I consent and run
  To every mire,
  And by this world's ill-guiding light,
  Err more than I can do by night.

  There is in God (some say)
A deep, but dazzling darkness, as men here   50
Say it is late and dusky, because they
  See not all clear.
  Oh for that night! where I in him
  Might live invisible and dim.

Corruption

Sure it was so. Man in those early days
  Was not all stone and earth;
He shined a little, and by those weak rays
  Had some glimpse of his birth.
He saw Heaven o'er his head, and knew from whence
  He came (condemnèd) hither;
And, as first love draws strongest, so from hence
  His mind sure progressed thither.
Things here were strange unto him: sweat and till,

All was a thorn or weed: 10
Nor did those last, but (like himself) died still
　　As soon as they did seed.
They seemed to quarrel with him; for that act
　　That felled him, foiled them all:
He drew the curse upon the world, and cracked
　　The whole frame with his fall.
This made him long for home, as loth to stay
　　With murmurers and foes;
He sighed for Eden, and would often say,
　　"Ah! what bright days were those!"   20
Nor was Heaven cold unto him; for each day
　　The valley or the mountain
Afforded visits, and still paradise lay
　　In some green shade or fountain.
Angels lay lieger here; each bush and cell,
　　Each oak and highway knew them;
Walk but the fields, or sit down at some well,
　　And he was sure to view them.
Almighty Love! where art thou now? Mad man
　　Sits down and freezeth on;   30
He raves, and swears to stir nor fire, nor fan,
　　But bids the thread be spun.
I see, thy curtains are close-drawn; thy bow
　　Looks dim too in the cloud;
Sin triumphs still, and man is sunk below
　　The center, and his shroud.
All's in deep sleep, and night; thick darkness lies
　　And hatcheth o'er thy people;
But hark! What trumpet's that? What angel cries
　　"Arise! Thrust in thy sickle."

Man

　Weighing the steadfastness and state
Of some mean things which here below reside,
Where birds like watchful clocks the noiseless date
　　And intercourse of times divide;

Where bees at night get home and hive, and flowers
  Early, as well as late,
Rise with the sun, and set in the same bowers;

 I would, said I, my God would give
The staidness of these things to man! for these
To His divine appointments ever cleave,   10
 And no new business breaks their peace;
The birds nor sow nor reap, yet sup and dine;
  The flowers without clothes live,
Yet Solomon was never dressed so fine.

 Man hath still either toys or care;
He hath no root, nor to one place is tied,
But ever restless and irregular
 About this earth doth run and ride;
He knows he hath a home, but scarce knows where;
  He says it is so far   20
That he hath quite forgot how to go there.

 He knocks at all doors, strays and roams,
Nay, hath not so much wit as some stones have,
Which in the darkest nights point to their homes
 By some hid sense their Maker gave;
Man is the shuttle, to whose winding quest
  And passage through these looms
God ordered motion, but ordained no rest.

"They are all gone into the world of light"

They are all gone into the world of light!
 And I alone sit lingering here;
Their very memory is fair and bright,
 And my sad thoughts doth clear.

It glows and glitters in my cloudy breast
 Like stars upon some gloomy grove,
Or those faint beams in which this hill is dressed,
 After the sun's remove.

I see them walking in an air of glory,
 Whose light doth trample on my days;   10
My days, which are at best but dull and hoary,
 Mere glimmerings and decays.

O holy hope, and high humility,
 High as the heavens above!
These are your walks, and you have showed them me
 To kindle my cold love.

Dear, beauteous death! the jewel of the just,
 Shining nowhere but in the dark;
What mysteries do lie beyond thy dust,
 Could man outlook that mark!   20

He that hath found some fledged bird's nest may know
 At first sight if the bird be flown;
But what fair well or grove he sings in now,
 That is to him unknown.

And yet, as angels in some brighter dreams
 Call to the soul when man doth sleep,
So some strange thoughts transcend our wonted themes
 And into glory peep.

If a star were confined into a tomb,
 Her captive flames must needs burn there;   30
But when the hand that locked her up gives room,
 She'll shine through all the sphere.

O Father of eternal life, and all
 Created glories under thee!
Resume thy spirit from this world of thrall
 Into true liberty!

Either disperse these mists, which blot and fill
 My pèrspective (still) as they pass,
Or else remove me hence unto that hill,
 Where I shall need no glass.   40

Ascension Hymn

Dust and clay,
Man's ancient wear!
Here you must stay,
But I elsewhere;
Souls sojourn here, but may not rest;
Who will ascend, must be undressed.

And yet some
That know to die
Before death come,
Walk to the sky   10
Even in this life; but all such can
Leave behind them the old man.

If a star
Should leave the sphere,
She must first mar
Her flaming wear,
And after fall, for in her dress
Of glory, she cannot transgress.

Man of old
Within the line   20
Of Eden could
Like the sun shine
All naked, innocent and bright,
And intimate with Heav'n, as light;

But since he
That brightness soiled,
His garments be
All dark and spoiled,
And here are left as nothing worth,
Till the refiner's fire breaks forth.   30

[Henry Vaughan] 120

Then comes he!
Whose mighty light
Made his clothes be
Like Heav'n, all bright;
The fuller, whose pure blood did flow
To make stained man more white than snow.

He alone
And none else can
Bring bone to bone
And rebuild man,   40
And by his all-subduing might
Make clay ascend more quick than light.

The World

I saw eternity the other night
Like a great ring of pure and endless light,
 All calm, as it was bright;
And round beneath it, time, in hours, days, years,
 Driven by the spheres,
Like a vast shadow moved, in which the world
 And all her train were hurled.
The doting lover in his quaintest strain
 Did there complain;
Near him, his lute, his fancy, and his flights,   10
 Wit's sour delights,
With gloves and knots, the silly snares of pleasure,
 Yet his dear treasure,
All scattered lay, while he his eyes did pour
 Upon a flower.

The darksome statesman, hung with weights and woe,
Like a thick midnight fog, moved there so slow
 He did not stay, nor go;
Condemning thoughts (like sad eclipses) scowl
 Upon his soul,   20
And clouds of crying witnesses without

Pursued him with one shout.
Yet digged the mole, and lest his ways be found,
    Worked under ground,
Where he did clutch his prey. But one did see
    That policy:
Churches and altars fed him; perjuries
    Were gnats and flies;
It rained about him blood and tears, but he
    Drank them as free.   30

The fearful miser on a heap of rust
Sat pining all his life there, did scarce trust
    His own hands with the dust;
Yet would not place one piece above, but lives
    In fear of thieves.
Thousands there were as frantic as himself,
    And hugged each one his pelf:
The downright epicure placed Heav'n in sense,
    And scorned pretense;
While others, slipped into a wide excess,   40
    Said little less;
The weaker sort, slight trivial wares enslave,
    Who think them brave;
And poor, despisèd truth sat counting by
    Their victory.

Yet some, who all this while did weep and sing,
And sing and weep, soared up into the ring;
    But most would use no wing.
"O fools!" said I, "thus to prefer dark night
    Before true light,   50
To live in grots and caves, and hate the day
    Because it shows the way,
The way which from this dead and dark abode
    Leads up to God,
A way where you might tread the sun, and be
    More bright than he."
But as I did their madness so discuss,
    One whispered thus:
"This ring the Bridegroom did for none provide,
    But for his bride."   60

"And do they so?"

ROMANS 8: 19

*Etenim res creatœ exerto capite observantes
expectant revelationem Filiorum Dei.*

And do they so? Have they a sense
    Of aught but influence?
Can they their heads lift, and expect,
    And groan too? Why th' elect
Can do no more; my volumes said
    They were all dull, and dead;
They judged them senseless, and their state
    Wholly inanimate.
    Go, go, seal up thy looks,
      And burn thy books.   10

I would I were a stone, or tree,
    Or flow'r by pedigree,
Or some poor highway herb, or spring
    To flow, or bird to sing!
Then should I (tied to one sure state)
    All day expect my date;
But I am sadly loose, and stray
    A giddy blast each way;
    O let me thus range!
      Thou canst not change.   20

Sometime I sit with thee and tarry
    An hour or so, then vary;
Thy other creatures in this scene
    Thee only aim and mean;
Some rise to seek thee, and with heads
    Erect peep from their beds;
Others, whose birth is in the tomb,
    And cannot quit the womb,
    Sigh there, and groan for thee,
      Their liberty.   30

O let me not do less! shall they
    Watch, while I sleep or play?
Shall I thy mercies still abuse
    With fancies, friends, or news?
O brook it not! thy blood is mine,
    And my soul should be thine;
O brook it not! why wilt thou stop,
    After whole showers, one drop?
    Sure, thou wilt joy to see
      Thy sheep with thee.   40

Love and Discipline

Since in a land not barren still
(Because thou dost thy grace distil)
My lot is fallen, blest be thy will!

And since these biting frosts but kill
Some tares in me which choke, or spill
That seed thou sow'st, blest be thy skill!

Blest be thy dew, and blest thy frost,
And happy I to be so crossed,
And cured by crosses at thy cost.

The dew doth cheer what is distressed,   10
The frosts ill weeds nip and molest;
In both thou work'st unto the best.

Thus while thy sev'ral mercies plot,
And work on me now cold, now hot,
The work goes on and slacketh not;

For as thy hand the weather steers,
So thrive I best, 'twixt joys and tears,
And all the year have some green ears.

The Dwelling-Place

ST. JOHN 1:38–39

What happy, secret fountain,
Fair shade or mountain,

[Henry Vaughan] 124

Whose undiscovered virgin glory
Boasts it this day, though not in story,
Was then thy dwelling? Did some cloud,
Fixed to a tent, descend and shroud
My distressed Lord? Or did a star,
Beckoned by thee, though high and far,
In sparkling smiles haste gladly down
To lodge light, and increase her own?   10
My dear, dear God! I do not know
What lodged thee then, nor where, nor how;
But I am sure, thou dost now come
Oft to a narrow, homely room,
Where thou too hast but the least part:
My God, I mean my sinful heart.

Thomas Traherne

The Salutation

These little limbs,
These eyes and hands which here I find,
These rosy cheeks wherewith my life begins,
Where have ye been? Behind
What curtain were ye from me hid so long!
Where was, in what abyss, my speaking tongue?

When silent I
So many thousand, thousand years
Beneath the dust did in a chaos lie,
How could I smiles or tears,   10
Or lips or hands or eyes or ears perceive?
Welcome ye treasures which I now receive.

I that so long
Was nothing from eternity,
Did little think such joys as ear or tongue
To celebrate or see:
Such sounds to hear, such hands to feel, such feet,
Beneath the skies on such a ground to meet.

New burnished joys,
Which yellow gold and pearls excel!   20
Such sacred treasures are the limbs in boys,
In which a soul doth dwell;
Their organized joints, and azure veins
More wealth include than all the world contains.

From dust I rise,
And out of nothing now awake;
These brighter regions which salute mine eyes,
A gift from God I take.
The earth, the seas, the light, the day, the skies,
The sun and stars are mine, if those I prize.   30

> Long time before
>   I in my mother's womb was born,
> A God, preparing, did this glorious store,
>   The world, for me adorn.
> Into this Eden so divine and fair,
> So wide and bright, I come His son and heir.

>   A stranger here
>   Strange things doth meet, strange glories see;
> Strange treasures lodged in this fair world appear,
>   Strange all and new to me.   40
> But that they mine should be, who nothing was,
> That strangest is of all, yet brought to pass.

Dumbness

> Sure man was born to meditate on things,
> And to contemplate the eternal springs
> Of God and nature, glory, bliss and pleasure,
> That life and love might be his heavenly treasure;
> And therefore speechless made at first, that he
> Might in himself profoundly busied be;
> And not vent out, before he hath ta'en in
> Those antidotes that guard his soul from sin.
>   Wise nature made him deaf too, that he might
> Not be disturbed, while he doth take delight   10
> In inward things, nor be depraved with tongues,
> Nor injured by the errors and the wrongs
> That *mortal words* convey. For sin and death
> Are most infused by accursed breath,
> That flowing from corrupted entrails, bear
> Those hidden plagues that souls alone may fear.
>   This, my dear friends, this was my blessed case;
> For nothing spoke to me but the fair face
> Of Heav'n and earth, before my self could speak,
> *I then my bliss did, when my silence, break.*   20
> My non-intelligence of human words
> Ten thousand pleasures unto me affords;
> For while I knew not what they to me said,

Before their souls were into mine conveyed,
Before that living vehicle of wind
Could breathe into me their infected mind,
Before my thoughts were leavenèd with theirs, before
There any mixture was; the holy door,
Or gate of souls was closed, and mine being one
Within it self to me alone was known.   30
Then did I dwell within a world of light,
Distinct and separate from all men's sight,
Where I did feel strange thoughts, and secrets see
That were, or seemed, only revealed to me;
There I saw all the world enjoyed by one;
There I was in the world my self alone;
No business serious seemed but one; no work
But one was found; and that did in me lurk.
      D'ye ask me what? It was with clearer eyes
To see all creatures full of deities;   40
Especially one's self; and to admire
The satisfaction of all true desire;
'Twas to be pleased with all that God hath done;
'Twas to enjoy *even all* beneath the sun;
'Twas with a steady and immediate sense
To feel and measure all the excellence
Of things; 'twas to inherit endless treasure,
And to be filled with everlasting pleasure;
To reign in silence, and to sing alone,
To see, love, covet, have, enjoy and praise, in one;   50
To prize and to be ravished; to be true,
Sincere and single in a blessed view
Of all his gifts. Thus was I pent within
A fort, impregnable to any sin:
Till the avenues being open laid,
Whole legions entered, and the forts betrayed.
Before which time a pulpit in my mind,
A temple, and a teacher I did find,
With a large text to comment on. No ear
But eyes them selves were all the hearers there.   60
And every stone, and every star a tongue,
And every Gale of wind a curious song.
The heavens were an oracle, and spake

[*Thomas Traherne*]   128

Divinity; the earth did undertake
The office of a priest; and I being dumb
(Nothing besides was dumb) all things did come
With voices and instructions; but when I
Had gained a tongue, their power began to die.
Mine ears let other noises in, not theirs.
A noise disturbing all my songs and prayers.   70
My foes pulled down the temple to the ground,
They my adoring soul did deeply wound,
And casting that into a swoon, destroyed
The oracle, and all I there enjoyed.
And having once inspired me with a sense
Of foreign vanities, they march out thence
In troops that cover and despoil my coasts,
Being the invisible, most hurtful hosts.
  Yet the first words mine infancy did hear,
The things which in my dumbness did appear,   80
Preventing all the rest, got such a root
Within my heart, and stick so close unto't,
It may be trampled on, but still will grow,
And nutriment to soil it self will owe.
The first impressions are immortal all;
And let mine enemies whoop, cry, roar, call,
Yet these will whisper if I will but hear,
And penetrate the heart, if not the ear.

Wonder

 How like an angel came I down!
  How bright are all things here!
When first among his works I did appear
 Oh, how their glory me did crown?
The world resembled his eternity,
  In which my soul did walk;
 And everything that I did see
   Did with me talk.

 The skies in their magnificence,
  The lively, lovely air,   10

Oh, how divine, how soft, how sweet, how fair!
    The stars did entertain my sense,
And all the works of God so bright and pure,
      So rich and great did seem,
   As if they must endure
      In my esteem.

A native health and innocence
      Within my bones did grow,
And while my God did all His glories show,
   I felt a vigor in my sense   20
That was all spirit. I within did flow
      With seas of life, like wine;
  I nothing in the world did know
      But 'twas divine.

Harsh ragged objects were concealed,
      Oppressions, tears, and cries,
Sins, griefs, complaints, dissensions, weeping eyes
  Were hid, and only things revealed
Which heavenly spirits and the angels prize.
      The state of innocence   30
  And bliss, not trades and poverties,
      Did fill my sense.

The streets were paved with golden stones;
      The boys and girls were mine,
Oh, how did all their lovely faces shine!
    The sons of men were holy ones,
Joy, beauty, welfare did appear to me,
      And everything which here I found,
  While like an angel I did see,
      Adorned the ground.   40

Rich diamond and pearl and gold
      In every place was seen;
Rare splendors, yellow, blue, red, white, and green,
  Mine eyes did everywhere behold;
Great wonders clothed with glory did appear,
      Amazement was my bliss,

That and my wealth was everywhere;
    No joy to this!

Cursed and devised proprieties,
    With envy, avarice,   50
And fraud, those fiends that spoil even Paradise,
    Flew from the splendor of mine eyes.
And so did hedges, ditches, limits, bounds:
    I dreamed not aught of those,
But wandered over all men's grounds,
        And found repose.

Proprieties themselves were mine,
    And hedges ornaments;
Walls, boxes, coffers, and their rich contents
    Did not divide my joys, but shine.   60
Clothes, ribbons, jewels, laces, I esteemed
    My joys by others worn:
For me they all to wear them seemed
        When I was born.

Hosanna

No more shall walls, no more shall walls confine
That glorious soul which in my flesh doth shine;
    No more shall walls of clay or mud
        Nor ceilings made of wood,
    Nor chrystal windows, bound my sight,
    But rather shall admit delight.
        The skies that seem to bound
            My joys and treasures,
        Or more endearing pleasures
        Themselves become a ground: 10
While from the center to the utmost sphere
My goods are multiplied ev'ry where.

The Deity, the Deity to me
Doth all things give, and make me clearly see
    The moon and stars, the air and sun

Into my chamber come;
The seas and rivers hither flow,
Yea, here the trees of Eden grow,
The fowls and fishes stand,
Kings and their thrones,   20
As 'twere, at my command;
God's wealth, his holy ones,
The ages too, and angels all conspire;
While I, that I the center am, admire.

No more, no more shall clouds eclipse my treasures,
Nor viler shades obscure my highest pleasures;
No more shall earthen husks confine
My blessings which do shine
Within the skies, or else *above;*
Both worlds one Heaven made by love,   30
In common happy I
With angels walk
And there my Joys espy;
With God himself I talk;
Wond'ring with ravishment all things to see
Such *real* joys, so truly *mine*, to be.

No more shall trunks and dishes be my store,
Nor ropes of pearl, nor chains of golden ore;
As if such beings yet were not,
They all shall be forgot.   40
No such in Eden did appear,
No such in Heaven: Heaven here
Would be, were those removed;
The sons of men
Live in Jerusalem,
Had they not baubles loved.
These clouds dispersed, the Heavens clear I see.
Wealth new-invented, *mine* shall never be.

Transcendent objects doth my God provide,
In such convenient order all contrived,   50
That all things in their proper place
My soul doth best embrace,
[*Thomas Traherne*] 132

Extends its arms beyond the seas,
Above the Heavens its self can please,
  With God enthroned may reign:
    Like sprightly streams
  My thoughts on things remain;
  Or else like vital beams
They reach to, shine on, quicken things, and make
Them truly useful; while I *all* partake.   60

For me the world created was by love;
For me the skies, the seas, the sun, do move;
  The earth for me doth stable stand;
    For me each fruitful land
  For me the very angels God make *His*
  And *my* companions in Bliss;
    His laws command all men
      That they love me,
    Under a penalty
    Severe, in case they miss;   70
His laws require His creatures all to praise
His name, and when they do't be most my joys.

"Contentment is a sleepy thing"

  Contentment is a sleepy thing!
    If it in death alone must die;
A quiet mind is worse than poverty!
    Unless it from enjoyment spring!
That's blessedness alone that makes a king!
Wherein the joys and treasures are so great,
They all the powers of the soul employ,
    And fill it with a work complete,
      While it doth all enjoy.
True joys alone contentment do inspire,   10
Enrich content, and make our courage higher.
    Content alone's a dead and silent stone:
      The real life of bliss
    Is glory reigning in a throne,
      Where all enjoyment is.

      ["*Contentment is a sleepy thing*"] 133

The soul of man is so inclin'd to see,
Without his treasures no man's soul can be
    Nor rest content uncrowned!
        Desire and love
Must in the height of all their rapture move,   20
    Where there is true felicity.
Employment is the very life and ground
Of life it self; whose pleasant motion is
        The form of bliss:
All blessedness a life with glory crowned.
Life! Life is all: in its most full extent
Stretched out to all things, and with all content!

On News

    News from a foreign country came,
As if my treasure and my wealth lay there;
    So much it did my heart inflame!
'Twas wont to call my soul into mine ear,
        Which thither went to meet
           The approaching sweet,
      And on the threshold stood
To entertain the unknown good
      It hovered there
      As if 'twould leave mine ear,   10
And was so eager to embrace
The joyful tidings as they came,
'Twould almost change its dwelling-place
    To entertain the same.

    As if the tidings were the things
My very joys themselves, my foreign treasure,
    Or else did bear them on their wings,
With so much joy they came, with so much pleasure.
      My soul stood at the gate
        To re-create   20
      Itself with bliss, and to
Be pleased with speed: A fuller view
      It fain would take,

Yet journeys back would make
Unto my heart, as if 'twould fain
Go out to meet, yet stay within,
To fit a place, to entertain
    And bring the tidings in.

What sacred instinct did inspire
My soul in childhood with an hope so strong?   30
    What secret force moved my desire
T' expect my joys beyond the seas, so young?
      Felicity I knew
        Was out of view;
      And being left alone,
I thought all happiness was gone
      From me! for this
      I thirsted for absent bliss,
Deeming that sure beyond the seas,
Or else in something near at hand   40
Yet, I knew not (since nought did please
    I knew) my bliss did stand.

But little did the infant dream
That all the treasures of the world were by,
    And that himself was so the cream
And crown of all, which round about did lie.
      Yet thus it was! The gem,
        The diadem,
      The ring enclosing all
That stood upon this earthy ball,   50
      The heav'nly eye,
      Much wider than the sky,
Wherein they all included were,
The glorious soul that was the king
Made to possess them, did appear
    A small and little thing.

Insatiableness II

This busy, vast, inquiring soul
    Brooks no control,

No limits will endure,
Nor any rest; it will all see,
Not time alone, but ev'n eternity.
What is it? Endless, sure.

'Tis mean ambition to desire
A single world;
To many I aspire,
Though one upon another hurled;   10
Nor will they all, if they be all confined,
Delight my mind.

This busy, vast, inquiring soul
Brooks no control;
'Tis hugely curious too.
Each one of all those worlds must be
Enriched with infinite variety
And worth, or 'twill not do.

'Tis nor delight nor perfect pleasure
To have a purse   20
That hath a bottom in its treasure,
Since I must thence endless expense disburse.
Sure there's a God, for else there's no delight,
One infinite.

On Leaping Over the Moon

I saw new worlds beneath the water lie,
New people; and another sky
And sun, which seen by day
Might things more clear display.
Just such another
Of late my brother
Did in his travel see, and saw by night
A much more strange and wondrous sight;
Nor could the world exhibit such another
So great a sight, but in a brother.   10

[Thomas Traherne] 136

Adventure strange! No such in story we
    New or old, true or feignèd, see.
        On earth he seemed to move,
        Yet heaven went above;
           Up in the skies
           His body flies
In open, visible, yet magic, sort;
    As he along the way did sport,
Like Icarus over the flood he soars
    Without the help of wing or oars.   20

As he went tripping o'er the king's highway,
    A little pearly river lay,
        O'er which, without a wing
        Or oar, he dared to swim,
           Swim through the air
           On body fair;
He would not trust Icarian wings,
    Lest they should prove deceitful things;
For had he fall'n, it had been wondrous high,
    Not from, but from above, the sky.   30

He might have dropped through that thin element
    Into a fathomless descent;
        Unto the nether sky
        That did beneath him lie,
           And there might tell
           What wonders dwell
On earth above. Yet doth he briskly runs
    And, bold, the danger overcomes:
Who, as he leapt, with joy related soon
    How *happy he* o'erleapt the moon.   40

What wondrous things upon the earth are done
    Beneath, and yet above, the sun?
        Deeds all appear again
        In higher spheres; remain
           In clouds as yet,
           But there they get
        [*On Leaping Over the Moon*]   137

Another light, and in another way
    Themselves to us *above* display.
The skies themselves this earthly globe surround;
    We're even here within them found.   50

On heav'nly ground within the skies we walk,
    And in this middle center talk:
        Did we but wisely move,
        On earth in heav'n above,
            We then should be
            Exalted high
Above the sky; from whence whoever falls,
    Through a long dismal precipice,
Sinks to the deep abyss where Satan crawls,
    Where horrid death and déspair lies.   60

As much as others thought themselves to lie
    Beneath the moon, so much more high
        Himself he thought to fly
        Above the starry sky,
            As *that* he spied
            Below the tide.
Thus did he yield me in the shady night
    A wondrous and instructive light,
Which taught me that under our feet there is
    As o'er our heads, a place of bliss.   70

Poverty

        As in the house I sate,
        Alone and desolate,
    No creature but the fire and I,
The chimney and the stool, I lift mine eye
            Up to the wall,
        And in the silent hall
            Saw nothing mine
    But some few cups and dishes shine,
The table and the wooden stools
        Where people used to dine;   10

A painted cloth there was,
Wherein some ancient story wrought
A little entertained my thought
Which light discovered through the glass.

I wondered much to see
That all my wealth should be
Confined in such a little room,
Yet hope for more I scarcely durst presume.
It grieved me sore
That such a scanty store   20
Should be my all;
For I forgot my ease and health,
Nor did I think of hands or eyes,
Nor soul nor body prize;
I neither thought the sun,
Nor moon, nor stars, nor people, *mine*,
Though they did round about me shine;
And therefore was I quite undone.

Some greater things, I thought,
Must needs for me be wrought,   30
Which till my craving mind could see
I ever should lament my poverty;
I fain would have
Whatever bounty gave,
Nor could there be
Without or love or Deity;
For, should not He be infinite
Whose hand created me?
Ten thousand absent things
Did vex my poor and absent mind,   40
Which, till I be no longer blind,
Let me not see the king of kings.

His love must surely be
Rich, infinite, and free;
Nor can he be thought a God
Of grace and power, that fills not his abode,
His holy court,

> In kind and liberal sort;
> Joys and pleasures,
> Plenty of jewels, goods, and treasures,   50
> (To enrich the poor, cheer the forlorn)
> His palace must adorn,
> And given all to me;
> For till *his* works *my* wealth became,
> No love or peace did me inflame:
> But now I have a Deity.

Walking

> To *walk* abroad is, not with eyes,
> But thoughts, the fields to see and prize;
> Else may the silent feet,
> Like logs of wood,
> Move up and down, and see no good,
> Nor joy nor glory meet.
>
> Ev'n carts and wheels their place do change,
> But cannot see, though very strange
> The glory that is by;
> Dead puppets may   10
> Move in the bright and glorious day,
> Yet not behold the sky.
>
> And are not men than they more blind,
> Who having eyes yet never find
> The bliss in which they move:
> Like statues dead
> They up and down are carrièd,
> Yet neither see nor love.
>
> To *walk* is by a thought to go;
> To move in spirit to and fro;   20
> To mind the good we see;
> To taste the sweet;
> Observing all the things we meet
> How choice and rich they be.

[*Thomas Traherne*]   140

To note the beauty of the day,
And golden fields of corn survey;
    Admire the pretty flow'rs
        With their sweet smell;
To praise their maker, and to tell
    The marks of his great pow'rs.   30

To fly abroad like active bees,
Among the hedges and the trees,
    To cull the dew that lies
        On ev'ry blade,
From ev'ry blossom; till we lade
    Our *minds*, as they their *thighs*.

Observe those rich and glorious things,
The rivers, meadows, woods, and springs,
    The fructifying sun;
        To note from far   40
The rising of each twinkling star,
    For us his race to run.

A little child these well perceives,
Who, tumbling in green grass and leaves,
    May rich as kings be thought;
        But there's a sight
Which perfect manhood may delight,
    To which we shall be brought.

While in those pleasant paths we talk,
'Tis *that* tow'rds which at last we walk;   50
    For we may by degrees
        Wisely proceed
Pleasures of love and praise to heed,
    From viewing herbs and trees.

The Rapture

    Sweet infancy!
O fire of Heaven! O sacred light!

How fair and bright!
How great am I,
Whom the whole world doth magnify!

O heavenly joy!
O great and sacred blessedness,
   Which I possess!
   So great a joy
Who did into my arms convey?   10

From God above
Being sent, the Heavens me inflame,
   To praise his name
   The stars do move!
The burning sun doth show his love.

Oh, how divine
Am I! To all this sacred wealth,
   This life and health,
   Who raised? Who mine
Did make the same? What hand divine?

Edmund Waller

Of English Verse

Poets may boast, as safely vain,
Their works shall with the world remain;
Both, bound together, live or die,
The verses and the prophecy.

But who can hope his lines should long
Last in a daily changing tongue?
While they are new, envy prevails;
And as that dies, our language fails.

When architects have done their part,
The matter may betray their art;   10
Time, if we use ill-chosen stone,
Soon brings a well-built palace down.

Poets that lasting marble seek
Must carve in Latin or in Greek;
We write in sand, our language grows,
And, like the tide, our work o'erflows.

Chaucer his sense can only boast,
The glory of his numbers lost!
Years have defaced his matchless strain,
And yet he did not sing in vain.   20

The beauties which adorned that age,
The shining subjects of his rage,
Hoping they should immortal prove,
Rewarded with success his love.

This was the generous poet's scope,
And all an English pen can hope,
To make the fair approve his flame,

That can so far extend their fame.

Verse, thus designed, has no ill fate
If it arrive but at the date
Of fading beauty; if it prove
But as long-lived as present love.

To Mr. Henry Lawes

WHO HAD THEN NEWLY SET A SONG OF MINE,
IN THE YEAR 1635

Verse makes heroic virtue live;
But you can life to verses give.
As when in open air we blow,
The breath, though strained, sounds flat and low;
But if a trumpet take the blast,
It lifts it high, and makes it last:
So in your airs our numbers dressed,
Make a shrill sally from the breast
Of nymphs, who, singing what we penned,
Our passions to themselves commend; 10
While love, victorious with thy art,
Governs at once their voice and heart.
    You, by the help of tune and time,
Can make that song which was but rhyme.
Noy pleading, no man doubts the cause;
Or questions verses set by Lawes.
    As a church window, thick with paint,
Lets in a light but dim and faint,
So others, with division, hide
The light of sense, the poet's pride; 20
But you alone may truly boast
That not a syllable is lost:
The writer's and the setter's skill
At once the ravished ears do fill.
Let those which only warble long,
And gargle in their throats a song,
Content themselves with *ut, re, mi:*
Let words, and sense, be set by thee.

[*Edmund Waller*] 144

Song

Stay, Phœbus! stay:
The world to which you fly so fast,
Conveying day
From us to them, can pay your haste
With no such object, nor salute your rise,
With no such wonder as De Mornay's eyes.

Well does this prove
The error of those antique books,
Which made you move
About the world; her charming looks   10
Would fix your beams, and make it ever day,
Did not the rolling earth snatch her away.

To A Very Young Lady

Why came I so untimely forth
Into a world which, wanting thee,
Could entertain us with no worth
Or shadow of felicity,
That time should me so far remove
From that which I was born to love?

Yet, fairest blossom! do not slight
That age which you may know so soon;
The rosy morn resigns her light,
And milder glory, to the noon;   10
And then what wonders shall you do,
Whose dawning beauty warms us so?

Hope waits upon the flowery prime;
And summer, though it be less gay,
Yet is not looked on as a time
Of declination or decay;

For with a full hand that does bring
All that was promised by the spring.

Go, Lovely Rose

Go, lovely rose!
Tell her that wastes her time and me
  That now she knows,
When I resemble her to thee,
  How sweet and fair she seems to be.

Tell her that's young,
And shuns to have her graces spied,
  That hadst thou sprung
In deserts, where no men abide,
  Thou must have uncommended died.   10

Small is the worth
Of beauty from the light retired;
  Bid her come forth,
Suffer herself to be desired,
  And not blush so to be admired.

Then die! that she
The common fate of all things rare
  May read in thee;
How small a part of time they share,
  That are so wondrous sweet and fair!   20

When He Was at Sea

Whilst I was free I wrote with high conceit,
And love and beauty raised above their height;
Love, that bereaves us both of brain and heart,
Sorrow and silence doth at once impart.
What hand at once can wield a sword and write
Or battle paint, engaged in the fight?
Who will describe a storm must not be there:

[Edmund Waller] 146

Passion writes well, neither in love nor fear.
Why on the naked boy have poets then
Feathers and wings bestowed, that wants a pen?   10

At Penshurst

Had Sacharissa lived when mortals made
Choice of their deities, this sacred shade
Had held an altar to her power, that gave
The peace and glory which these alleys have;
Embroidered so with flowers where she stood,
That it became a garden of a wood.
Her presence has such more than human grace,
That it can civilize the rudest place;
And beauty too, and order, can impart,
Where nature ne'er intended it, nor art.   10
The plants acknowledge this, and her admire,
No less than those of old did Orpheus' lyre;
If she sit down, with tops all towards her bowed,
They round about her into arbors crowd;
Or if she walk, in even ranks they stand,
Like some well marshalled and obsequious band.
Amphion so made stones and timber leap
Into fair figures from a confused heap;
And in the symmetry of her parts is found
A power like that of harmony in sound.   20
  Ye lofty beeches, tell this matchless dame
That if together ye fed all one flame,
It could not equalize the hundredth part
Of what her eyes have kindled in my heart!
Go, boy, and carve this passion on the bark
Of yonder tree, which stands the sacred mark
Of noble Sidney's birth; when such benign,
Such more than mortal-making stars did shine,
That there they cannot but for ever prove
The monument and pledge of humble love;   30
His humble love whose hopes shall ne'er rise higher,
Than for a pardon that he dares admire.

To the King, On His Navy

Where'er thy navy spreads her canvas wings,
Homage to thee, and peace to all she brings;
The French and Spaniard, when thy flags appear,
Forget their hatred, and consent to fear.
So Jove from Ida did both hosts survey,
And when he pleased to thunder, part the fray.
Ships heretofore in seas like fishes sped,
The mighty still upon the smaller fed;
Thou on the deep imposest nobler laws,
And by that justice hast removed the cause   10
Of those rude tempests, which for rapine sent,
Too oft, alas! involved the innocent.
Now shall the ocean, as thy Thames, be free
From both those fates, of storms and piracy.
But we most happy, who can fear no force
But wingèd troops, or Pegasean horse.
'Tis not so hard for greedy foes to spoil
Another nation, as to touch our soil.
Should nature's self invade the world again,
And o'er the center spread the liquid main,   20
Thy power were safe, and her destructive hand
Would but enlarge the bounds of thy command;
Thy dreadful fleet would style thee lord of all,
And ride in triumph o'er the drownèd ball;
Those towers of oak o'er fertile plains might go,
And visit mountains where they once did grow.
    The world's restorer never could endure
That finished Babel should those men secure,
Whose pride designed that fabric to have stood   30
Above the reach of any second flood;
To thee, his chosen, more indulgent, he
Dares trust such power with so much piety.

Song

Say, lovely dream! where couldst thou find
    Shadows to counterfeit that face?

Colors of this glorious kind
Come not from any mortal place.

In heaven itself thou sure wert drest
  With that angel-like disguise:
  Thus deluded am I blest,
And see my joy with closèd eyes.

But, ah! this image is too kind
  To be other than a dream;   10
  Cruel Sacharissa's mind
Never put on that sweet extreme!

Fair dream! if thou intend'st me grace,
  Change that heavenly face of thine;
  Paint despised love in thy face,
And make it to appear like mine.

Pale, wan, and meager let it look,
  With a pity-moving shape,
  Such as wander by the brook
Of Lethe, or from graves escape.   20

Then to that matchless nymph appear,
  In whose shape thou shinest so;
  Softly in her sleeping ear,
With humble words, express my woe.

Perhaps from greatness, state, and pride,
  Thus surprisèd she may fall:
  Sleep does disproportion hide,
And, death resembling, equals all.

On a Girdle

That which her slender waist confined
Shall now my joyful temples bind;
No monarch but would give his crown,
His arms might do what this has done.

It was my heaven's extremest sphere,

The pale which held that lovely deer;
My joy, my grief, my hope, my love,
Did all within this circle move!

A narrow compass! and yet there
Dwelt all that's good, and all that's fair;   10
Give me but what this riband bound,
Take all the rest the sun goes round!

Of the Last Verses in the Book

When we for age could neither read nor write,
The subject made us able to indite;
The soul, with nobler resolutions decked,
The body stooping, does herself erect.
No mortal parts are requisite to raise
Her that, unbodied, can her Maker praise.
     The seas are quiet when the winds give o'er;
So, calm are we when passions are no more!
For then we know how vain it was to boast
Of fleeting things, so certain to be lost.   10
Clouds of affection from our younger eyes
Conceal that emptiness which age descries.
     The soul's dark cottage, battered and decayed,
Lets in new light through chinks that time has made;
Stronger by weakness, wiser, men become
As they draw near to their eternal home.
Leaving the old, both worlds at once they view,
That stand upon the threshold of the new.

John Wilmot, Earl of Rochester

Upon Drinking in a Bowl

Vulcan, contrive me such a cup
  As Nestor used of old:
Show all thy skill to trim it up;
  Damask it round with gold.

Make it so large, that, filled with sack
  Up to the swelling brim,
Vast toasts, on the delicious lake,
  Like ships at sea, may swim.

Engrave not battle on his cheek;
  With war I've nought to do: 10
I'm none of those that took Maestrick,
  Nor Yarmouth leaguer knew.

Let it no name of planets tell,
  Fixed stars, or constellations;
For I am no Sindrophel,
  Nor none of his relations.

But carve thereon a spreading vine;
  Then add two lovely boys;
Their limbs in amorous folds entwine,
  The type of future joys.   20

Cupid and Bacchus my saints are;
  May drink and love still reign:
With wine I wash away my cares,
  And then to love again.

A Song

Absent from thee I languish still,

Then ask me not when I return?
The straying fool 'twill plainly kill,
  To wish all day, all night to mourn.

Dear, from thine eyes then let me fly,
  That my fantastic mind may prove
The torments it deserves to try,
  That tears my fixed heart from my love.

When wearied with a world of woe
  To thy safe bosom I retire,   10
Where love, and peace, and truth does flow,
  May I contented there expire.

Lest once more wandering from that Heav'n,
  I fall on some base heart unblessed,
Faithless to thee, false, unforgiven,
  And lose my everlasting rest.

The Maimed Debauchee

As some brave Admiral, in former War
  Deprived of force, but pressed with courage still,
Two rival fleets appearing from afar,
  Crawls to the top of an adjacent hill

From whence (with thoughts full of concern) he views
  The wise and daring conduct of the fight,
And each bold action to his mind renews,
  His present glory, and his past delight.

From his fierce eyes flashes of rage he throws,
  As from black clouds when lightening breaks away, 10
Transported thinks himself amidst his Foes,
  And absent, yet enjoys the bloody day.

So when my days of impotence approach,
  And I'm by love and wine's unlucky chance,

Driv'n from the pleasing billows of debauch,
    On the dull shore of lazy temperance.

My pains at last some respite shall afford,
    While behold the battles you maintain:
When fleets of glasses sail around the board,
    From whose broad-sides volleys of wit shall rain.   20

Nor shall the sight of honorable scars,
    Which my too forward valor did procure,
Frighten new-listed soldiers from the wars,
    Past joys have more than paid what I endure.

Should some brave youth (worth being drunk) prove nice,
    And from his fair inviter meanly shrink,
'Twould please the ghost of my departed vice,
    If, at my counsel, he repent and drink.

Or should some cold-complexioned sot forbid,
    With his dull morals, our night's brisk alarms,   30
I'll fire his blood, by telling what I did,
    When I was strong, and able to bear arms.

I'll tell of whores attacked their lords at home,
    Bawds' quarters beaten up, and fortress won;
Windows demolished, watches overcome,
    And handsome ills by my contrivance done.

With tales like these I will such heat inspire,
    As to important mischief shall incline;
I'll make him long some ancient church to fire,
    And fear no lewdness they're called to by wine.   40

Thus statesman-like I'll saucily impose,
    And, safe from danger, valiantly advise;
Sheltered in impotence urge you to blows,
    And, being good for nothing else, be wise.

The Mistress

A SONG

An age, in her embraces past,
  Would seem a winter's day,
Where life and light, with envious haste
  Are torn and snatched away.

But, oh! how slowly minutes roll,
  When absent from her eyes,
That feed my love, which is my soul;
  It languishes and dies.

For then no more a soul but shade,
  It mournfully does move,   10
And haunts my breast, by absence made
  The living tomb of love.

You wiser men despise me not,
  Whose lovesick fancy raves,
On shades of souls, and Heav'n knows what;
  Short ages live in graves.

When e're those wounding eyes, so full
  Of sweetness you did see,
Had you not been profoundly dull,
  You had gone mad like me.   20

Nor censure us, you who perceive
  My best belov'd and me
Sigh and lament, complain and grieve;
  You think we disagree.

Alas! 'tis sacred jealousy,
  Love raised to an extreme:
The only proof 'twixt her and me,
  We love, and do not dream.

Fantastic fancies fondly move,
  And in frail joys believe,   30
Taking false pleasure for true love,
  But pain can ne'er deceive.

Kind jealous doubts, tormenting fears,
  And anxious cares, when past,
Prove our hearts' treasure fixed and dear,
  And make us bless'd at last.

Upon Nothing

Nothing! thou elder brother ev'n to shade,
That had'st a being e'er the world was made,
And (well fixed) art alone, of ending not afraid.

E'er time and place were, time and place were not,
When primitive Nothing something straight begot,
Then all proceeded from the great united—what.

Something, the gen'ral attribute of all,
Severed from thee, its sole original,
Into thy boundless self must undistinguished fall.

Yet something did thy mighty pow'r command,   10
And from thy fruitful emptiness' hand,
Snatched men, beasts, birds, fire, air and land.

Matter, the wicked'st offspring of thy race,
By form assisted, flew from thy embrace,
And rebel light obscured thy reverend dusky face.

With form, and matter, time and place did join,
Body, thy foe, with thee did leagues combine,
To spoil thy peaceful realm, and ruin all thy line.

But turncoat time assists the foe in vain,
And, bribed by thee, assists thy short-lived reign.   20
And to thy hungry womb drives back thy slaves again.

Though mysteries are barred from laick eyes,
And the divine alone, with warrant, pries
Into thy bosom, where the truth in private lies,

Yet this of thee the wise may freely say,
Thou from the virtuous nothing tak'st away,
And to be part with thee the wicked wisely pray.

Great negative, how vainly would the wise
Enquire, define, distinguish, teach, devise?
Didst thou not stand to point their dull philosophies. 30

Is, or is not, the two great ends of fate,
And, true or false, the subject of debate,
That perfect, or destroy, the vast designs of fate,

When they have racked the politician's breast,
Within thy bosom most securely rest,
And, when reduced to thee, are least unsafe and best.

But, Nothing, why does Something still permit,
That sacred monarchs should at council sit,
With persons highly thought at best for nothing fit,

Whilst weighty Something modestly abstains,   40
From princes' coffers, and from statesmen's brains,
And nothing there like stately Nothing reigns,

Nothing who dwell'st with fools in grave disguise,
For whom they rev'rend shapes, and forms devise,
Lawn sleeves, and furs, and gowns, when they like
    thee look wise.

French truth, Dutch prowess, British policy,
Hibernian learning, Scotch civility,
Spaniard's dispatch, Dane's wit, are mainly seen in thee.

The great man's gratitude to his best friend,
King's promises, whore's vows, towards thee they bend, 50
Flow swiftly into thee, and in thee ever end.

A Satyr against Mankind

   Where I (who to my cost already am
One of those strange, prodigious creatures, man)
A spirit free, to choose for my own share,
What case of flesh and blood I pleased to wear,
I'd be a dog, a monkey, or a bear,
Or any thing but that vain animal,
Who is so proud of being rational.
The senses are too gross, and he'll contrive
A sixth, to contradict the other five;
And before certain instinct, will prefer   10
Reason, which fifty times for one does err;
Reason, an *ignis fatuus*, in the mind,
Which leaving light of nature, sense, behind
Pathless and dang'rous wand'ring ways it takes,
Through errors, fenny bogs, and thorny brakes;
Whilst the misguided follower climbs with pain
Mountains of whimseys, heaped in his own brain;
Stumbling from thought to thought, falls headlong down,
Into doubt's boundless sea, where like to drown,
Books bear him up awhile, and makes him try   20
To swim with bladders of philosophy;
In hopes still to o'ertake th' escaping light,
The vapor dances in his dazzled sight,
Till spent, it leaves him to eternal night.
Then old age, and experience, hand in hand,
Lead him to death, and make him understand,
After a search so painful, and so long,
That all his life he has been in the wrong;
Huddled in dirt, the reas'ning engine lies,
Who was so proud, so witty, and so wise.   30
Pride drew him in, as cheats their bubbles catch,
And makes him venture to be made a wretch.
His wisdom did his happiness destroy,
Aiming to know what world he should enjoy;
And wit was his vain, frivolous pretense

Of pleasing others, at his own expense.
For wits are treated just like common whores:
First they're enjoyed, and then kicked out of doors;
The pleasure past, a threat'ning doubt remains,
That frights th' enjoyer with succeeding pains.   40
Women and men of wit are dang'rous tools,
And ever fatal to admiring fools:
Pleasure allures, and when the fops escape,
'Tis not that they're belov'd, but fortunate,
And therefore what they fear, at least they hate.
    But now methinks some formal band and beard
Takes me to task; come on, Sir, I'm prepared.
    "Then, by your favor, any thing that's writ
Against this gibing, jingling knack called wit
Likes me abundantly, but you take care   50
Upon this point, not to be too severe.
Perhaps my muse were fitter for this part,
For I profess, I can be very smart
On wit, which I abhor with all my heart;
I long to lash it in some sharp essay,
But your grand indiscretion bids me stay,
And turns my tide of ink another way.
What rage ferments in your degen'rate mind,
To make you rail at reason, and mankind?
Blessed, glorious man! to whom alone kind Heav'n   60
An everlasting soul has freely giv'n;
Whom his great maker took such care to make,
That from himself he did the image take,
And this fair frame in shining reason dressed,
To dignify his nature above beast;
Reason, by whose aspiring influence,
We take a flight beyond material sense,
Dive into mysteries, then soaring pierce
The flaming limits of the universe,
Search Heaven and Hell, find out what's acted there, 70
And give the world true grounds of hope and fear."
    Hold, mighty man, I cry, all this we know
From the pathetic pen of Ingello,
From P[atrick's] *Pilgrim*, S[ibbes'] soliloquies,
And 'tis this very reason I despise:

This supernatural gift, that makes a mite
Think he is the image of the infinite,
Comparing his short life, void of all rest,
To the eternal, and the ever blessed.
This busy, puzzling stirrer-up of doubt,   80
That frames deep mysteries, then finds 'em out,
Filling with frantic crowds of thinking fools
Those reverend bedlams, colleges and schools,
Borne on whose wings, each heavy sot can pierce
The limits of the boundless universe.
So charming ointments make an old witch fly,
And bear a crippled carcass through the sky.
'Tis this exalted pow'r, whose business lies
In nonsense and impossibilities.
This made a whimsical philosopher,   90
Before the spacious world, his tub prefer,
And we have modern cloistered coxcombs who
Retire to think, 'cause they have naught to do.
But thoughts are giv'n for action's government;
Where action ceases, thought's impertinent;
Our sphere of action is life's happiness,
And he who thinks beyond, thinks like an ass.
Thus, whilst 'gainst false reas'ning I inveigh,
I own right reason, which I would obey:
That reason that distinguishes by sense,   100
And gives us rules of good and ill from thence,
That bounds desires with a reforming will,
To keep 'em more in vigor, not to kill.
Your reason hinders, mine helps t' enjoy,
Renewing appetites yours would destroy.
My reason is my friend, yours is a cheat;
Hunger calls out, my reason bids me eat;
Perversely, yours your appetite does mock:
This asks for food, that answers, "What's o'clock?"
This plain distinction, sir, your doubt secures: 110
'Tis not true reason I despise, but yours.
Thus I think reason righted, but for man,
I'll ne'er recant, defend him if you can.
For all his pride, and his philosophy,
'Tis evident, beasts are in their degree,

[*A Satyr against Mankind*]   159

As wise at least, and better far than he.
Those creatures are the wisest who attain,
By surest means, the ends at which they aim.
If therefore Jowler finds and kills his hares
Better than M[eres] supplies committee chairs,   120
Though one's a statesman, th' other but a hound,
Jowler, in justice, would be wiser found.
You see how far man's wisdom here extends;
Look next, if human nature makes amends:
Whose principles most generous are, and just,
And to whose morals you would sooner trust.
Be judge yourself, I'll bring it to the test:
Which is the basest creature, man or beast?
Birds feed on birds, beasts on each other prey,
But savage man alone does man betray.   130
Pressed by necessity, they kill for food;
Man undoes man to do himself no good.
With teeth and claws by nature armed they hunt
Nature's allowances, to supply their want.
But man, with smiles, embraces, friendships, praise,
Inhumanly his fellow's life betrays;
With voluntary pains works his distress,
Not through necessity, but wantonness.
For hunger or for love they fight or tear,
Whilst wretched man is still in arms for fear;   140
For fear he arms, and is of arms afraid,
By fear, to fear, successively betrayed;
Base fear, the source whence his best passions came,
His boasted honor and his dear bought fame;
That lust of pow'r, to which he's such a slave,
And for the which alone he dares be brave;
To which his various projects are designed,
Which makes him gen'rous, affable, and kind;
For which he takes such pains to be thought wise,
And screws his actions, in a forced disguise,   150
Leading a tedious life in misery,
Under laborious, mean hypocrisy.
Look to the bottom of his vast design,
Wherein man's wisdom, pow'r, and glory join;

[*John Wilmot, Earl of Rochester*]   160

The good he acts, the ill he does endure,
'Tis all for fear, to make himself secure.
Merely for safety, after fame we thirst,
For all men would be cowards if they durst.
And honesty's against all common sense:
Men must be knaves, 'tis in their own defence.   160
Mankind's dishonest; if you think it fair,
Amongst known cheats, to play upon the square,
You'll be undone . . .
Nor can weak truth your reputation save:
The knaves will all agree to call you knave.
Wronged shall he live, insulted o'er, oppressed,
Who dares be less a villain than the rest.
Thus, sir, you see what human nature craves:
Most men are cowards, all men should be knaves.
The difference lies (as far as I can see)   170
Not in the thing itself, but the degree;
And all the subject matter of debate
Is only who's a knave of the first rate?

All this with indignation have I hurled
At the pretending part of the proud world,
Who, swoll'n with selfish vanity, devise
False freedoms, holy cheats, and formal lies
Over their fellow slaves to tyrannize.

But if in court so just a man there be
(In court a just man, yet unknown to me)   180
Who does his needful flattery direct,
Not to oppress and ruin, but protect,
Since flattery, which way so ever laid,
Is still a tax on that unhappy trade;
If so upright a statesman you can find,
Whose passions bend to his unbiassed mind,
Who does his arts and policies apply
To raise his country, not his family,
Nor, while his pride owned avarice withstands,
Receives aureal bribes, from friends' corrupted hands. 190

Is there a churchman who on God relies?
Whose life, his faith and doctrine justifies?
Not one blown up with vain prelatic pride,

[A Satyr against Mankind]   161

Who, for reproof of sins, does man deride;
Whose envious heart with his obstrep'rous
    saucy eloquence,
Dares chide at kings, and rail at men of sense;
Who from his pulpit vents more peevish lies,
More bitter railings, scandals, calumnies,
Than at a gossipping are thrown about,
When the good wives get drunk, and then fall out.   200
None of that sensual tribe whose talents lie
In avarice, pride, sloth, and gluttony;
Who hunt good livings, but abhor good lives;
Whose lust exalted, to that height arrives,
They act adultery with their own wives,
And ere a score of years completed be,
Can from the lofty pulpit proudly see
Half a large parish their own progeny.

    Nor doting B —— who would be adored,
For domineering at the council board,   210
A greater fop in business at fourscore,
Fonder of serious toys, affected more,
Than the gay, glitt'ring fool at twenty proves,
With all his noise, his tawdry clothes, and loves.

    But a meek, humble man of modest sense,
Who, preaching peace, does practice continence;
Whose pious life's a proof he does believe,
Mysterious truths, which no man can conceive.
If upon earth there dwell such God-like men,
I'll here recant my paradox to them,   220
Adore those shrines of virtue, homage pay,
And, with the rabble world, their laws obey.
If such there are, yet grant me this at least:
Man differs more from man, than man from beast.

Love and Life

A SONG

All my past life is mine no more,
    The flying hours are gone:
Like transitory dreams given o'er,

Whose images are kept in store,
  By memory alone.

The time that is to come, is not,
  How can it then be mine?
The present moment's all my lot,
And that, as fast as it is got,
  Phyllis, is only thine.   10

Then talk not of inconstancy,
  False hearts, and broken vows;
If I, by miracle, can be
This livelong minute true to thee,
  'Tis all that heaven allows.

Constancy

A SONG

I cannot change, as others do,
  Though you unjustly scorn,
Since that poor swain that sighs for you,
  For you alone was born.
No, Phyllis, no, your heart to move
  A surer way I'll try;
And to revenge my slighted love,
  Will still love on, will still love on, and die.

When killed with grief Amyntas lies,
  And you to mind shall call   10
The sighs that now unpitied rise,
  The tears that vainly fall,
That welcome hour that ends this smart,
  Will then begin your pain:
For such a faithful tender heart
  Can never break, can never break in vain.

A Song

Phillis, be gentler, I advise;
  Make up for time misspent,

When beauty on its death-bed lyes,
  'Tis high time to repent.

Such is the malice of your fate,
  That makes you old so soon;
Your pleasure ever comes too late,
  How early e'er begun.

Think what a wretched thing is she,
  Whose stars contrive, in spite,   10
The morning of her love should be
  Her fading beauty's night.

Then if, to make your ruin more,
  You'll peevishly be coy,
Die with the scandal of a whore,
  And never know the joy.

Plain Dealing's Downfall

Long time plain dealing in the haughty town,
Wand'ring about, though in thread-bare gown,
At last unanimously was cried down.

When almost starved, she to the country fled,
In hopes, though meanly she should there be fed,
And tumble nightly on a pea-straw bed.

But knav'ry knowing her intent, took post,
And rumored her approach through every coast,
Vowing his ruin that should be her host.

Frighted at this, each rustic shut his door,   10
Bid her be gone, and trouble him no more,
For he that entertained her must be poor.

At this grief seized her, grief too great to tell,
When weeping, sighing, fainting, down she fell,
While knavery, laughing, rung her passing bell.

        [*John Wilmot, Earl of Rochester*] 164

To Corinna

A SONG

What cruel pains Corinna takes,
 To force that harmless frown;
When not one charm her face forsakes,
 Love cannot lose his own.

So sweet a face, so soft a heart,
 Such eyes so very kind,
Betray, alas! the silly art
 Virtue had ill designed.

Poor feeble tyrant! who in vain
 Would proudly take upon her,   10
Against kind nature to maintain,
 Affected rules of honor.

The scorn she bears so helpless proves,
 When I plead passion to her,
That much she fears, (but more she loves,)
 Her vassal should undo her.

Edward Lord Herbert
   (1583–1648)

Elegy Over a Tomb

Must I then see, alas! eternal night
    Sitting upon those fairest eyes,
And closing all those beams, which once did rise
    So radiant and bright
That light and heat in them to us did prove
    Knowledge and love?

Oh, if you did delight no more to stay
    Upon this low and earthly stage,
But rather chose an endless heritage,
    Tell us at least, we pray,   10
Where all the beauties that those ashes owed
    Are now bestowed.

Doth the sun now his light with yours renew?
    Have waves the curling of your hair?
Did you restore unto the sky and air
    The red, and white, and blue?
Have you vouchsafed to flowers since your death
    That sweetest breath?

Had not Heav'n's lights else in their houses slept,
    Or to some private life retired?   20
Must not the sky and air have else conspired,
    And in their regions wept?
Must not each flower else the earth could breed
    Have been a weed?

But thus enriched may we not yield some cause
    Why they themselves lament no more,

That must have changed the course they held before,
    And broke their proper laws,
Had not your beauties giv'n this second birth
    To heaven and earth?   30

Tell us (for oracles must still ascend
    For those that crave them at your tomb),
Tell us where are those beauties now become,
    And what they now intend;
Tell us, alas, that cannot tell our grief,
    Or hope relief.

William Drummond
(1585–1649)

Madrigal I

This life which seems so fair
Is like a bubble blown up in the air
By sporting children's breath,
Who chase it everywhere,
And strive who can most motion it bequeath;
And though it sometime seem of its own might
(Like to an eye of gold) to be fixed there,
And firm to hover in that empty height,
That only is *because it is so light;*
But in that pomp it doth not long appear;   10
    For even when most admired, it in a thought,
    As swelled from nothing, doth dissolve in nought.

William Browne
(c. 1591–1643?)

"Down in a valley"

Down in a valley, by a forest's side,
Near where the crystal Thames rolls on her waves,
I saw a mushroom stand in haughty pride,
As if the lilies grew to be his slaves.
The gentle daisy, with her silver crown,
Worn in the breast of many a shepherd's lass;
The humble violet, that lowly down
Salutes the gay nymphs as they trimly pass;
These, with a many more, methought, complained
That nature should those needles things produce,   10
Which not alone the sun from others gained,
But turn it wholly to their proper use.
   I could not choose but grieve that nature made
   So glorious flowers to live in such a shade.

Phineas Fletcher
(1582–1650)

An Hymn

Drop, drop, slow tears,
   And bathe those beauteous feet
Which brought from heav'n
   The news and prince of peace,
Cease not, wet eyes,
   His mercies to entreat;

To cry for vengeance
    Sin doth never cease;
In your deep floods
    Drown all my faults and fears,   10
Nor let his eye
    See sin, but through my tears.

George Wither
    (1588–1667)

Sonnet 4

Shall I, wasting in despair,
Die because a woman's fair?
Or make pale my cheeks with care,
'Cause another's rosy are?
Be she fairer than the day,
Or the flow'ry meads in May,
    If she be not so to me,
    What care I, how fair she be.

Shall my heart be grieved or pined
'Cause I see a woman kind?   10
Or a well-disposèd nature
Joinèd with a lovely feature?
Be she meeker, kinder than
Turtledove or pelican,
    If she be not so to me,
    What care I, how kind she be.

Shall a woman's virtues move
Me to perish for her love?
Or, her well-deserving known,
Make me quite forget mine own?   20
Be she with that goodness blest
Which may gain her name of best,

If she be not such to me,
What care I, though great she be.

'Cause her fortune seems too high,
Shall I play the fool and die?
Those that bear a noble mind,
Where they want of riches find,
Think, what with them, they would do
That without them, dare to woo   30
  And unless that mind I see,
  What care I though great she be.

Great, or good, or kind, or fair,
I will ne'er the more despair;
If she love me, this believe,
I will die, ere she shall grieve.
If she slight me when I woo,
I can scorn, and let her go;
  For if she be not for me,
  What care I, for whom she be.   40

Richard Corbet
(1582–1632)

To His Son, Vincent Corbet, On His Birthday

BEING THEN THREE YEARS OLD

What I shall leave thee none can tell,
But all shall say I wish thee well:
I wish thee, Vin, before all wealth,
Both bodily and ghostly health;
Nor too much wealth, nor wit, come to thee,
So much of either may undo thee.
I wish thee learning, not for show,
Enough for to instruct, and know;
Not such as gentlemen require,

To prate at table, or at fire.
I wish thee all thy mother's graces,
Thy father's fortunes, and his places.
I wish thee friends, and one at court,
Not to build on, but support,
To keep thee, not in doing many
Oppressions, but from suffering any.
I wish thee peace in all thy ways,
Nor lazy nor contentious days;
And when thy soul and body part,
As innocent as now thou art.

William Strode
(1601?–1645)

On Chloris Walking in the Snow

I saw fair Chloris walk alone
Where feathered rain came softly down,
Then Jove descended from his tower
To court her in a silver shower;
The wanton snow flew to her breast
Like little birds into their nest,
But overcome with whiteness there
For grief it thawed into a tear,
Then falling down her garment hem
For grief it freezed into a gem.

Aurelian Townshend
(c. 1583–1642)

A Dialogue Betwixt Time and a Pilgrim

Pilgr. Aged man, that mows these fields.
Time. Pilgrim speak, what is thy will?

[*A Dialogue Betwixt Time and a Pilgrim*] **171**

Pilgr. Whose soil is this that such sweet pasture yields?
   Or who art thou whose foot stand never still?
   Or where am I? *Time.* In love.
Pilgr. His lordship lies above.
Time. Yes and below, and round about
   Where in all sorts of flow'rs are growing
  Which as the early spring puts out,
   Time falls as fast a mowing.
Pilgr. If thou art time, these flow'rs have lives,
   And then I fear,
  Under some lilly she I love
   May now be growing there.
Time. And in some thistle or some spire of grass,
  My scythe thy stalk before hers come may pass.
Pilgr. Will thou provide it may? *Time.* No.
Pilgr. Allege the cause.
Time. Because time cannot alter but obey fate's laws.
Cho. Then happy those whom fate, that is the stronger,
  Together twists their threads, and yet draws hers
   the longer.

William Cartwright
(1611–1643)

No Platonic Love

Tell me no more of minds embracing minds,
  And hearts exchanged for hearts;
That spirits spirits meet, as winds do winds,
  And mix their subtlest parts;
That two unbodied essences may kiss,
And then like angels, twist and feel one bliss.

I was that silly thing that once was wrought
  To practise this thin love;

I climbed from sex to soul, from soul to thought;
    But thinking there to move,   10
Headlong I rolled from thought to soul, and then
From soul I lighted at the sex again.

As some strict down-looked men pretend to fast
    Who yet in closets eat,
So lovers who profess they spirits taste,
    Feed yet on grosser meat;
I know they boast they souls to souls convey,
Howe'er they meet, the body is the way.

Come, I will undeceive thee: they that tread
    Those vain aerial ways   20
Are like young heirs and alchemists, misled
    To waste their wealth and days;
For searching thus to be forever rich,
They only find a med'cine for the itch.

Francis Quarles
(1592–1644)

A Good-Night

Close now thine eyes, and rest secure;
Thy soul is safe enough, thy body sure;
        He that loves thee, he that keeps
And guards thee, never slumbers, never sleeps.
The smiling conscience in a sleeping breast
        Has only peace, has only rest;
        The music and the mirth of kings,
Are all but very discords, when she sings;
        Then close thine eyes and rest secure;
No sleep so sweet as thine, no rest so sure.

Thomas Stanley
(1625–1678)

Expectation

Chide, chide no more away
The fleeting daughters of the day,
Nor with impatient thoughts out-run
    The lazy sun,
Or think the hours do move too slow;
    Delay is kind,
  And we too soon shall find,
That which we seek, yet fear to know.

The mystic dark decrees
Unfold not of the destinies,   10
Nor boldly seek to antedate
    The laws of fate;
Thy anxious search awhile forbear,
    Suppress thy haste,
  And know that time at last
Will crown thy hope, or fix thy fear.

Sidney Godolphin
(1610–1643)

Song

Or love me less, or love me more
  And play not with my liberty,
Either take all, or all restore,

Bind me at least, or set me free;
Let me some nobler torture find
  Than of a doubtful wavering mind;
Take all my peace, but you betray
  Mine honor too this cruel way.

'Tis true that I have nursed before
  That hope of which I now complain,   10
And having little, sought no more,
  Fearing to meet with your disdain;
The sparks of favor you did give,
  I gently blew to make them live;
And yet have gained by all this care
  No rest in hope, nor in despair.

I see you wear that pitying smile
  Which you have still vouchsafed my smart,
Content thus cheaply to beguile
  And entertain an harmless heart;   20
But I no longer can give way
  To hope, which doth so little pay,
And yet I dare no freedom owe
  Whilst you are kind, though but in show.

Then give me more, or give me less,
  Do not disdain a mutual sense,
Or your unpitying beauties dress
  In their own free indifference;
But show not a severer eye
  Sooner to give me liberty,   30
For I shall love the very scorn
  Which for my sake you do put on.

James Shirley
  (*1596–1666*)

"*The glories of our blood and state*"

The glories of our blood and state,
    ["*The glories of our blood and state*"]   175

Are shadows, not substantial things,
There is no armor against fate,
   Death lays his icy hand on Kings;
      Scepter and crown,
      Must tumble down,
And in the dust be equal made,
With the poor crooked scythe and spade.

Some men with swords may reap the field,
   And plant fresh laurels where they kill,   10
But their strong nerves at last must yield,
   They tame but one another still;
      Early or late,
      They stoop to fate,
And must give up the murmuring breath,
When they, pale captives, creep to death.

The garlands wither on your brow,
   Then boast no more your mighty deeds;
Upon death's purple altar now,
   See where the victor-victim bleeds,   20
      Your heads must come,
      To the cold tomb;
Only the actions of the just
Smell sweet, and blossom in their dust.

John Cleveland
(1613–1658)

Mark Antony

Whenas the nightingale chanted her vespers,
And the wild forester couched on the ground,
Venus invited me in th' evening whispers
Unto a fragrant field with roses crowned,

Where she before had sent
My wishes' complement;
Unto my heart's content
Played with me on the green.
  Never Mark Antony
  Dallied more wantonly   10
  With the fair Egyptian Queen.

First on her cherry cheeks I mine eyes feasted,
Thence fear of surfeiting made me retire;
Next on her warmer lips, which when I tasted,
My duller spirits made active as fire.
  Then we began to dart,
  Each at another's heart,
  Arrows that knew no smart,
  Sweet lips and smiles between.
    Never Mark, &c.   20

Wanting a glass to plait her amber tresses,
Which like a bracelet rich deckèd mine arm,
Gaudier than Juno wears whenas she graces
Jove with embraces more stately than warm;
  Then did she peep in mine
  Eyes' humor crystalline;
  I in her eyes was seen,
  As if we one had been.
    Never Mark, &c.

Mystical grammar of amorous glances;   30
Feeling of pulses, the physic of love;
Rhetorical courtings and musical dances;
Numb'ring of kisses arithmetic prove;
  Eyes like astronomy;
  Straight-limbed geometry;
  In her art's ingeny
  Our wits were sharp and keen.
    Never Mark Antony
    Dallied more wantonly
    With the fair Egyptian Queen.   40

Sir William Davenant
(1606–1668)

The Philosopher and the Lover
To a Mistress Dying

LOVER.

Your beauty, ripe, and calm, and fresh
  As eastern summers are,
Must now, forsaking time and flesh,
  Add light to some small star.

PHILOSOPHER.

Whilst she yet lives, were stars decayed,
  Their light by hers relief might find;
But death will lead her to a shade
  Where love is cold, and beauty blind.

LOVER.

Lovers, whose priests all poets are,
  Think ev'ry mistress when she dies   10
Is changed at least into a star;
  And who dares doubt the poets wise?

PHILOSOPHER.

But ask not bodies doomed to die
  To what abode they go;
Since knowledge is but sorrow's spy,
  It is not safe to know.

Sir John Denham
(1615–1669)

On Mr. Abraham Cowley, His Death and Burial Amongst the Ancient Poets

Old Chaucer, like the morning star,
To us discovers day from far;
His light those mists and clouds dissolved,
Which our dark nation long involved;
But he descending to the shades,
Darkness again the age invades.
Next (like Aurora) Spenser rose,
Whose purple blush the day foreshows;
The other three with his own fires,
Phœbus, the poets' god, inspires: 10
By Shakespeare's, Jonson's, Fletcher's lines,
Our stage's luster Rome's outshines.
These poets near our princes sleep,
And in one grave their mansion keep;
They lived to see so many days,
Till time had blasted all their bays;
But cursed be the fatal hour
That plucked the fairest, sweetest flower
That in the Muses' garden grew,
And amongst withered laurels threw.   20
Time, which made them their fame outlive,
To Cowley scarce did ripeness give.
Old mother wit and nature gave
Shakespeare and Fletcher all they have;
In Spenser and in Jonson, art
Of slower nature got the start;
But both in him so equal are,
None knows which bears the happiest share;
To him no author was unknown,

Yet what he wrote was all his own; 30
He melted not the ancient gold,
Nor with Ben Jonson did make bold
To plunder all the Roman stores
Of poets and of orators;
Horace his wit, and Virgil's state,
He did not steal, but emulate,
And when he would like them appear,
Their garb, but not their clothes, did wear.
He not from Rome alone, but Greece,
Like Jason brought the golden fleece; 40
To him that language (though to none
Of th' others) as his own was known.
On a stiff gale, as Flaccus sings,
The Theban swan extends his wings,
When through th' ethereal clouds he flies;
To the same pitch our swan doth rise—
Old Pindar's flights by him are reached,
When on that gale his wings are stretched.
His fancy and his judgment such,
Each to the other seemed too much, 50
His severe judgment, giving law,
His modest fancy kept in awe,
As rigid husbands jealous are
When they believe their wives too fair.
His English stream so pure did flow
As all that saw and tasted know;
But for his Latin vein so clear,
Strong, full and high, it doth appear
That were immortal Virgil here,
Him, for his judge, he would not fear; 60
Of that great portraiture, so true
A copy pencil never drew.
By muse her song had ended here,
But both their genii straight appear;
Joy and amazement her did strike,
Two twins she never saw so like.
'Twas taught by wise Pythagoras,
One soul might through more bodies pass;
Seeing such transmigration here,

She thought it not a fable there— 70
Such a resemblance of all parts,
Life, death, age, fortune, nature, arts;
Then lights her torch at theirs, to tell
And show the world this parallel.
Fixed and contemplative their looks
Still turning over nature's books;
Their works chaste, moral, and divine,
Where profit and delight combine;
They, gilding dirt, in noble verse
Rustic philosophy rehearse. 80
When heroes, gods, or god-like kings
They praise, on their exalted wings
To the celestial orbs they climb,
And with the harmonious spheres keep time.
Nor did their actions fall behind
Their words, but with like candor shined;
Each drew fair characters, yet none
Of these they feigned, excels their own.
Both by two generous princes loved,
Who knew and judged what they approved; 90
Yet having each the same desire,
Both from the busy throng retire.
Their bodies to their minds resigned,
Cared not to propagate their kind;
Yet though both fell before their hour,
Time on their offspring hath no power;
Nor fire nor fate their bays shall blast,
Nor death's dark veil their day o'ercast.

John Norris
(1657–1711)

The Retirement

Well, I have thought on't, and I find
This busy world is nonsense all;

I here despair to please my mind,
Her sweetest honey is so mixed with gall.
Come then, I'll try how 'tis to be alone,
Live to my self a while, and be my own.

I've tried, and bless the happy change;
So happy, I could almost vow
Never from this retreat to range,
For sure I ne'er can be so blessed as now.   10
From all th'allays of bliss I here am free,
I pity others, and none envy me.

Here in this shady lonely grove,
I sweetly think my hours away,
Neither with business vex'd, nor love,
Which in the world bear such tyrannic sway:
No tumults can my close apartment find,
Calm as those seats above, which know no storm nor
        wind.

Let plots and news embroil the state,
Pray, what's that to my books and me?   20
Whatever be the kingdom's fate,
Here I am sure t' enjoy a monarchy.
Lord of my self, accountable to none,
Like the first man in Paradise, alone.

While the ambitious vainly sue,
And of the partial stars complain,
I stand upon the shore and view
The mighty labors of the distant main;
I'm flushed with silent joy, and smile to see
The shafts of fortune still drop short of me.   30

Th' uneasy pageantry of state,
And all the plagues of thought and sense
Are far removed; I'm placed by fate
Out of the road of all impertinence.
Thus, though my fleeting life runs swiftly on,
'Twill not be short, because 'tis all my own.

Sir Charles Sedley
(1638–1701)

Song

Phillis is my only joy,
   Faithless as the winds or seas;
Sometimes coming, sometimes coy,
   Yet she never fails to please;
     If with a frown
     I am cast down,
     Phillis smiling,
     And beguiling,
Makes me happier than before.

Though, alas, too late I find,   10
   Nothing can her fancy fix;
Yet the moment she is kind,
   I forgive her all her tricks;
     Which, though I see,
     I can't get free;
     She deceiving,
     I believing;
What can lovers wish for more?

Sir George Etherege
(1635?–1691)

Silvia

The nymph that undoes me, is fair and unkind,
No less than a wonder by nature designed;

[*Silvia*]   183

She's the grief of my heart, the joy of my eye,
And the cause of a flame that never can die.

Her mouth from whence wit still obligingly flows
Has the beautiful blush, and smell of the rose;
Love and destiny both attend on her will,
She wounds with a look, with a frown she can kill.

The desperate lover can hope no redress,
Where beauty and rigor are both in excess;   10
In Silvia they meet, so unhappy am I,
Who sees her must love, and who loves her must die.

Charles Sackville, Earl of Dorset
   (1638–1706)

Song

May the ambitious ever find
   Success in crowds and noise,
While gentle love does fill my mind
   With silent real joys;

May knaves and fools grow rich and great,
   And the world think 'em wise;
While I lie dying at her feet,
   And all the world despise.

Let conquering kings new triumphs raise,
   And melt in court delights: 10
Her eyes can give much brighter days,
   Her arms much softer nights.

Notes

HENRY KING

UPON THE DEATH OF MY EVER-DESIRED FRIEND, DOCTOR DONNE, DEAN OF PAUL'S

Line 8: *pin it:* this was literally done.

Lines 29–34: refer to Donne's last sermon, "Death's Duel," preached before the King in 1630 and described by Isaak Walton in his *Life of Dr. Donne* (1640).

Line 40: *prevent:* anticipate.

THE EXEQUY

King's first wife, Anne, died c. 1624.

SIC VITA

Appeared first in Francis Beaumont's *Poems* (1640), but is generally attributed to King.

A CONTEMPLATION UPON FLOWERS

was not included in the 1657 edition but appears in a manuscript signed "H. Kinge."

THE CHANGE

The subtitle is a Spanish motto meaning: "The wise man changes consciously; the fool (or rather, madman) perseveres."

THE RETREAT

Line 6: *rack:* fly, as vapor or broken clouds.

THOMAS CAREW

AN ELEGY UPON THE DEATH OF DOCTOR DONNE, DEAN OF PAUL'S

Line 5: *unscissored:* with uncut hair.

Line 66: *Metamorphoses:* referring to the vogue for Ovid's poems.

INGRATEFUL BEAUTY THREATENED

Line 6: *imped:* from falconry, to repair an injured wing by grafting feathers.

IN ANSWER OF AN ELEGIACAL LETTER UPON THE DEATH OF THE KING OF SWEDEN

Line 2: *Barbican:* the name of a London street (where Townshend lived) meaning "outer fortification."

Line 5: *Sweden's fall:* death of Gustavus Adolphus in 1632.

Lines 19–21: names of places, rivers, generals connected with Gustavus' campaigns.

Line 24: *The Knight o' the Sun:* hero of a popular romance.

Line 25: *grave chronicler:* Tacitus, whose *Annals* recorded deeds of the Caesars.

Line 43: *Caesar:* Emperor Ferdinand II, leader of Catholics.

Line 44: *United Princes:* Protestant Union.

Line 54: *Shepherd's Paradise:* a pastoral comedy by Walter Montague.

Lines 58–88: description of Townshend's mask, *Tempe Restored.*

TO MY WORTHY FRIEND, MASTER GEORGE SANDYS, ON HIS TRANSLATION OF THE PSALMS

George Sandys (1578-1644), famous traveller and translator, was notable for his use of the closed, balanced couplet.

TO BEN JONSON

The New Inne, produced in 1629, was hissed off the stage. Jonson's *Ode* of defiance was published with the play in 1631.

Line 31: *Goodwin frame:* quicksands along the Kentish coast.

SIR JOHN SUCKLING

A BALLAD UPON A WEDDING

Line 1: *Dick:* a typical rustic name.

Line 12: *Vorty:* rustic dialect for "forty."

Line 19: *course-a-park:* country game in which a girl calls on a man to chase her.

Line 79: In the 1646 edition, this stanza (with its two halves inverted) comes after line 96. The generally preferred order followed here is that of the 1648 and later editions.

SONNET III

Line 23: *Sophonisba,* daughter of Carthaginian general, Hasdrubel.

Lines 26–28: names of characters in Sidney's *Arcadia*.

RICHARD LOVELACE

TO ALTHEA, FROM PRISON

Line 17: *committed:* caged.

THE SNAIL

Line 14: *Preventing:* anticipating.

Line 31: *cubs of India:* animals thought to protect their young by hiding them in a hanging pouch of skin.

Line 43: *Scythians:* referring to their nomadic ways.

THE GRASSHOPPER

Charles Cotton (1630–1687), a poet, for whose first marriage Lovelace wrote *The Triumphs of Philamore and Amoret* in 1656.

Line 10: *plats:* plots.

Line 31: *old Greek:* old Greek wine.

LA BELLA BONA ROBA

Title: harlot.

Line 15: *rascal deer:* lean deer.

TO LUCASTA. THE ROSE

Line 14: *Silenus:* foster-father of Bacchus and leader of satyrs.

Line 10: *blow-god's:* probably Aeolus, god of winds.

ABRAHAM COWLEY

ON THE DEATH OF MR. CRASHAW

Line 20: see I Kings 12: xxv–xxxiii.

Line 28: *fabulous:* given to fables.

Line 40: Crashaw died a convert at Loreto, where he had been given a post at the shrine.

Line 55: *nice:* subtle.

Line 66–67: see II Kings 2: ix–xi.

ON THE DEATH OF MR. WILLIAM HERVEY

Latin quotation: from *Epigrams* 6: xxix of Martial, epigrammatist of the first century A.D.: "To those extraordinarily gifted, life is short, and old age rare."

Line 17: see II Samuel 18: xxxiii: David's lament for Absalom.

Line 35: *Ledæn stars:* Castor and Pollux, twin sons of Leda and Zeus, were placed together in the heavens because of their great love for each other.

Line 71: When Cyparissus, a beautiful youth loved by Apollo, died of grief at accidentally killing a pet stag, Apollo transformed him into a cypress.

ODE. OF WIT

Line 2: *Thou:* unidentified, but it has been suggested that the reference is to Thomas Sprat (1635–1713), Bishop of Rochester, propagandist for the Royal Society, who was also Cowley's biographer and editor.

Line 12: *Zeuxis' birds:* referring to the remarkably lifelike painting style of Zeuxis of Heraclea, Greek painter of the end of the fifth century.

Line 29: *numbers:* music of Amphion, which charmed the stones into their places in the Theban wall.

Line 50: *Bajazet:* conquered emperor in Marlow's *Tamburlaine*.

Line 52: *short-lunged Seneca:* refers to vogue for so-called Senecan style, composed of short, abrupt members, broken by many pauses.

RICHARD CRASHAW

UPON TWO GREEN APRICOTS SENT TO COWLEY BY SIR CRASHAW

These lines apparently accompanied two poems by Crashaw that he sent to his poet-friend.

Line 3: *Pomona:* goddess of fruit trees.

Line 12: Cowley's first volume, *Poetical Blossoms,* was published when he was only thirteen years old.

Line 30: *Hesperides:* garden producing the golden apples.

WISHES TO HIS (SUPPOSED) MISTRESS

Lines 88–90: refer to elegant conversations in Sidney's *Arcadia.*

IN THE HOLY NATIVITY OF OUR LORD GOD

Line 98: the month of May was supposed to have been named after the goddess Maia, mother of Hermes.

TO THE NOBLEST AND BEST OF LADIES, THE COUNTESS OF DENBIGH

The Countess of Denbigh was one of Queen Henrietta Maria's ladies of the bedchamber.

A HYMN TO THE NAME AND HONOR OF THE ADMIRABLE SAINT TERESA

Subtitle: *Discalced:* barefoot.

Line 71: *rase:* cut, slash.

Line 79: refers to St. Teresa's vision of an angel thrusting a golden dart into her heart.

UPON BISHOP ANDREWES, HIS PICTURE BEFORE HIS SERMONS

Lancelot Andrewes (1555–1626), leading Anglican bishop (of Chichester, then Ely, and finally Westminster), one of the translators of the King James' Version of the Bible, was renowned for his learning, eloquence, and piety.

HENRY VAUGHAN

REGENERATION

Line 28: see Genesis 28: x–xxii.

THE NIGHT

Line 5: see John 2: iii.

CORRUPTION

Line 25: *lieger*: as ambassador.

"THEY ARE ALL GONE INTO THE WORLD OF LIGHT"

Line 5: *It*: the memory.

ASCENSION HYMN

Line 12: *old man*: old Adam. See Romans 6: vi.

"AND DO THEY SO?"

Romans 8: xix: "For the earnest expectation of the creature waiteth for the manifestation of the sons of God."

THOMAS TRAHERNE

For discussion of textual problems, especially of changes made by Traherne's editor, his brother Philip, see H. M. Margoliouth's introduction and notes to *Thomas Traherne's Centuries, Poems, and Thanksgivings* (Oxford, 1958).

WONDER

Line 49: *proprieties*: proprietorship.

INSATIABLENESS II

Line 15: *curious*: fastidious.

EDMUND WALLER

TO MR. HENRY LAWES

Henry Lawes (1595–1662), one of the most famous

English composers of the century, wrote the music for Milton's *Comus*.

Line 15: *Noy:* William Noy, well-known lawyer, became attorney general in 1631.

SONG: "Stay, Phœbus!"

Line 6: *De Mornay:* probably the name of a French-woman in Queen Henrietta Maria's train.

AT PENSHURST

Line 17: *Amphion:* Zeus' son, whose music magically moved the stones that formed the walls of Thebes.

SONG: "Say, lovely dream!"

Line 20: *Lethe:* stream in the lower world from which the shades drank to forget the past.

JOHN WILMOT, EARL OF ROCHESTER

UPON DRINKING IN A BOWL

A free adaptation of the eighteenth ode of the Greek poet, Anacreon (563?–478 B.C.).

Line 2: see *Iliad*, xi: 632ff.

Line 11: *Maestrick:* taken by the French and English in 1673.

Line 12: *Yarmouth leaguer:* English man-of-war used as besieger.

Line 15: *Sindrophel:* astrologer satirized in Samuel Butler's *Hudibras* (1678).

A SATYR AGAINST MANKIND

Satyr: One Renaissance theory of the derivation of "satire" was that it was the genre of poems which by their rough, crude character might appropriately be spoken by a satyr.

Line 31: *bubbles:* dupes.

Line 46: *band:* Geneva band worn by parsons.

Line 73: *Ingello:* Nathaniel Ingello, author of *Bentivolio and Urania*, an allegorical romance.

Line 74: *P[atrick's] Pilgrim: The Parable of a Pilgrim,*

a religious allegory by Simon Patrick, Bishop of Ely. *S[ibbes'] soliloquies:* Richard Sibbes was the author of numerous long religious discourses.

Line 90: *whimsical philosopher:* Diogenes, the Cynic.

Line 120: *M[eres]:* Sir Thomas Meres, M. P. for Lincoln under Charles II, Commissioner for the Admiralty (1679–1684).

Line 209: *doting B ——:* possibly Thomas Barlow (1607–1691), Bishop of Lincoln.

MISCELLANY

John Cleveland, MARK ANTONY

Line 36: *ingeny:* ingenuity, wit.

Sir John Denham, ON MR. ABRAHAM COWLEY, HIS DEATH AND BURIAL

Line 43: *Flaccus:* Latin poet Horace (Quintus Horatius Flaccus, 65–8 B.C.).

Line 44: *Theban swan:* Pindar (522–448 B.C.?), Greek lyric poet whose odes Cowley imitated and adapted in his English Pindaric odes.

Line 64: *both their genii:* Virgil's and Cowley's.

Lines 79–80: referring to Virgil's *Georgics* and Cowley's adaptations of that genre of bucolic poetry.